GROWING UP
Vick

Sam + Marilyn
+ Yael;

It was such a
pleasure meeting you!
Continue Blessings

Thanks A Million
Tina Liberti

GROWING UP Vick

A Story of
"The Strength and Resilience of the Vick Family"

WRITTEN BY

TINA VICK

AUNT OF NATIONAL FOOTBALL LEAGUE SUPERSTAR
MICHAEL VICK

FOREWORD WRITTEN BY AUTHOR'S DAUGHTER,
TEUNSHA VICK

EDITED BY
CHARRITA D. DANLEY

COVER DESIGN BY SHAWN GARY,
MINDOFAGENIUS DESIGNWORKS,
WWW.MOAGONLINE.COM

authorHOUSE®

AuthorHouse™
1663 Liberty Drive
Bloomington, IN 47403
www.authorhouse.com
Phone: 1-800-839-8640

Published by AuthorHouse   06/17/2013

ISBN: 978-1-4772-9111-5 (sc)
ISBN: 978-1-4772-9110-8 (hc)
ISBN: 978-1-4772-9109-2 (e)

Library of Congress Control Number: 2012921616

Any people depicted in stock imagery provided by Thinkstock are models, and such images are being used for illustrative purposes only.
Certain stock imagery © Thinkstock.

This book is printed on acid-free paper.

Because of the dynamic nature of the Internet, any web addresses or links contained in this book may have changed since publication and may no longer be valid. The views expressed in this work are solely those of the author and do not necessarily reflect the views of the publisher, and the publisher hereby disclaims any responsibility for them.

Book Credits
"Daily Press"
CNN sportsillustrated.cnn.com/football/college/1999/bowls/sugar/news, "Sugar Bowl Notebook"

DISCLOSURE

The copy of this manuscript is for the publishers at Authorhouse Publishing and for them only. Please do not send to any other publisher.

TABLE OF CONTENTS

ACKNOWLEDGEMENTS

Sitting here in disbelief that I have finally finished this book, I have mixed emotions. I owe and many thanks to the people who have kept me inspired. First and foremost, I thank God for giving me the vision and the strength to complete the book. I thank my two wonderful children, Teunsha Lynette and Terrance Leonard who are the "true" loves of my life. They have been the two people on earth who have helped me tremendously. And the matriarch of the Vick family, my mother, Caletha Vick, who was not here on earth during my writing, but her spirit has been strong and has strengthened me throughout this process. I cherish my three grandsons, Shamar, Tyree and Tyson, who didn't want me to write this book, when it was time for us to play at King-Lincoln Park. Those three wouldn't take any excuses. Thank you to my special daughter in law, Shameka Harris, for her support. Kudos also goes to my family members who believed I could do it. I want to thank Marlon Carter, with Airbrush Fanatics, and Marlon Jr. for all of their kind words of inspiration. To Sam Reynolds and his wife, who guided me every step of the way. Delphine and Carl White, I thank you for the countless hours of edits and revisions. Many thanks to my special friends, John Eley, Carolyn Johnson, Chris Taylor, Erica Wagner, Andrew Shannon, Dr. Karen Turner Ward and her daughter, Jade Banks, and Dr. Patricia Woodbury for all of their critiques and ideas. A special thanks to the photographer, Jerry Taliaferro, for allowing me to use his photograph of me, and to *The Daily Press*, our local newspaper, for the photos.

INTRODUCTION

The foundation of who I am came from these two words: strength and resilience. There have been many trials throughout my life, but I have been able to continue to proceed and make my life a joy to live. However, I am well aware that my journey in life definitely didn't begin with me. Part of the reason I wrote this book was to celebrate the fortitude of my wonderful mother, Caletha Virginia Vick. I appreciate the love she spread throughout the Vick family, which taught me how to live with very few material possessions and have joy because of the love in my heart. The strength she had to raise six children was amazing! Her strength was also a part of the resiliency of my nephew, Michael Vick, as he faced many of his challenges. Because of the fibers in our DNA, the Vick family would overcome.

Writing this book has been one of the most difficult things I have ever done. I hope readers will understand my message of "pressing your way through," especially when others doubt you or think you don't even stand a chance. The ability to recover or adjust easily to misfortune or change helped create these chapters. We have persevered! I now have another item to add to my bucket list . . . my story of "Growing Up Vick."

FOREWORD

Through It All

By Teunsha Vick

Your wealth is not measured in material things
You don't have furs
Millions of dollars or diamond rings.
But your soul is as rich as they come
Thank you for all you've done
Because you should have given up
So thanks for thinking of us.
Through it All
You've made it Momma
Through it All, you didn't fall.
I will never be able to repay
How through all odds, you paved a way
You're so strong and so smart
You're the reason I embraced my art
For Years I've wondered how you made it through
And all of the trials never bothered you.
And as you rise and sometimes fall
But you've made it THROUGH IT ALL!

(My daughter wrote this at age 17. She is amazing!)

CHAPTER ONE

THE VICK MATRIARCH

Caletha Virginia Vick

The obituary read, "Our heavenly Father needed another Angel. On May 2, 2008, he sent for our beloved Caletha Virginia Vick." I just couldn't believe my Mother was gone. All five of my siblings—even my oldest brother Joseph—were sitting in Cooke Brothers Funeral Home at the homegoing service for the woman who loved us more than anyone on this great Earth.

Born to the late Mr. and Mrs. Samuel and Ada Glast on January 10, 1932, Momma was raised in Edgecombe County, located in the Eastern coastal plains of North Carolina along the Tar River. I never had a chance to meet Grandma Ada. They said she went blind in her forties, and later passed away. From the recollections of my mother, it sounded as if Grandma Ada had diabetes, which in the mid 1900's was not easily detected, and certainly not treated.

I will always remember the affectionate stories Momma would tell us about her mother. Grandma Ada was known as a faith healer in the bordering regions of Edgecombe County where both she and my mother grew up. My mother told us stories of how people would come to their house to get healed of different sicknesses or "ailments," as she called them. Since Grandma Ada's patients would be referred to now as "walk-ins," she insisted on keeping a fresh supply of materials on hand. One of my mother's daily chores included a trip into the woods with her brothers and sisters to pick plants, herbs, and berries. Grandma would then remedy her patients by serving them an herbal cocktail and berries. Momma would always laugh when she told us how people would sometimes go to the outhouse to find snakes and frogs coming out of their butts, but she assured us that meant the evil spirits were being released. During that time, there was no indoor plumbing, and an outhouse served as the toilet. Then Grandma Ada would read different scriptures from the Bible, touch them with her hands, and all of a sudden, they were HEALED!

After Momma graduated from public school in North Carolina, she met and married my father, Joseph Vick, in November 1951. Two years later my parents relocated to Newport News, Virginia. Newport News is a long stretch of land, 26 miles long from the north to the south.

There in Newport News, Virginia my parent's started the Vick Family. The first born was Joseph Vick Jr. and each year afterwards there was an addition to the Vick Family: Gwendolyn Diane, Joyce Reunise, Tina Leanne, Brenda Jean, and Casey Cardell. My mom and dad decided not to have any more children after Casey was born in 1963. We had a nice family from what I can remember. My dad worked at a place called Electronic Service while my mom stayed at home to raise us. Daddy was very handsome. He was brown skinned, 5' 11", with natural muscular build. I don't remember him exercising to keep in shape. He just had a muscular physique. Momma was a pretty, brown skinned and shapely lady. She had a tiny waist and large hips with big, pretty legs. Some of momma's friends from North Carolina called her "Red." But they didn't call her "Red" because of her skin color. She said it was because of the dusty red streak of hair in her head.

We lived in a housing development called the old Newsome Park. My dad made pretty good money, but I don't think he realized that the more children he had, the more money would be needed. All of us had huge appetites, and it was difficult to have enough money to feed the entire family.

"Joe, we need to get some more groceries for these children," Momma would tell daddy.

"Didn't we just go to the store to get food on Saturday?" he would ask.

"Yeah, but it's Wednesday and you know how these children eat."

"Well, I won't have any more money until Friday when I get paid," Daddy would say.

Momma would always finish the conversation by saying, "We need to figure out something, because I can't let these children go two days with no food."

Those were two things momma was going to figure out, how to get food for her children and how to get some darn cod liver oil.

"Come on Tina, Brenda and Casey! Come over here and take this so ya'll won't get a cold."

"Oh no, please momma!" we would beg in unison.

"Do we have to take it?" we questioned.

"I'm going to hide!" Brenda said as she ran towards the closet in the hallway.

"Ya'll stop acting like that; this stuff is not that bad and it will keep the colds away."

We could not stand it when momma pulled out that cod liver oil, but she assured us it would keep us from getting a cold. She would cut an orange in quarters and give us each a piece to suck on after she gave us the tablespoon of oil.

As soon as we took the spoonful of oil, we started screaming, "Gimme the orange! Gimme the orange!"

Neither of us would even think about swallowing that thick, smelly oil without having a piece of the orange in our hands. We would squeeze the orange and press it on our lips until there was no more juice. We used the juice to dilute the horrible taste of the cod liver oil. I have to admit we all stayed healthy and didn't get any colds. I know mom would not have put us through the torture of taking the disgusting oil, if she didn't think it would keep us healthy.

Even though I was young when we lived in Newsome Park, I do remember quite a few neighbors. There were a lot of families living there and everyone had at least five children. The adults who stood out in my mind are: Mrs. Lydia and her husband, Mr. Skipper; Mr. Townes and his wife whom everyone called Mrs. Bessie Rene; Mrs. Betty and Mr. Jasper; and Mrs. Sallie Mae. Momma said Mrs. Betty loved to hold me because she loved to look at my small nose. Momma always talked to Mrs. Sallie Mae, who used her cast iron skillet to protect momma, on nights when momma and daddy's discussions got out of control.

I also remember the apartment building. It had white wood siding with black shutters. It was a World War II housing project for black defense workers. It contained at least 2600 units, plus a school. The name came from Attorney Joseph Thomas Newsome who was born in Sussex County and moved to Newport News in 1904. He married his high school sweetheart, Mary B. Winfred, and they had one daughter. Attorney Newsome became a successful lawyer, political activist and speaker. It was a time when neighbors were true neighbors, and looked out for each other, and the residents enjoyed Newsome Park.

Friday nights were the best at our apartment. Mom always had the music playing with the best of Motown hits. We would always have dinner from a restaurant because daddy got paid on Fridays. There was a delivery place called Billy D's that had the best chili hotdogs with onions and some great tasting hamburgers and french fries. Sometimes we would have a barrel of Kentucky Fried Chicken original recipe or we would get take out Chinese food with pork fried rice, yock-a-mein and shrimp egg foo young. We'd have our dinner at the dinner table and there was always so much laughter and happiness. After we would eat, we would get on the floor and dance to songs of entertainers like Marvin Gaye, The Temptations, The Supremes and The Jackson Five. We also loved to watch "The Lawrence Welk Show" with his big band music and the bubbles floating around the stage at the end of the show. We thought it was amazing. We couldn't wait to see "The Ed Sullivan Show," and we would stay up late to watch it. Back in the 60's most television shows would not show the black acts like Otis Redding, Sammy Davis Jr. and James Brown until the end. My mother just loved to watch in amazement because she could not believe that black people were on television!

Over the next few years, life as we knew it became very difficult. Our family was constantly moving because daddy wouldn't keep the rent paid. I remember that his boss helped us get a house. It was three bedrooms and one bathroom at 406 Maple Avenue in an area called "The Creek." Coming home from work, daddy would usually stop at a bar, and then come home and pick a fight with momma about some of the smallest things. For example, if the dishes weren't dry or the food was too salty, daddy would start an argument. Soon after, he was throwing punches at mom.

Joe Jr. and Diane used to try to help my momma fight, but Brenda and I would run and hide in the closet. Sometimes we would stay in there for hours until we did not hear any more commotion. He would calm down after my brother and sister fought back. Once Diane hit him in the eye with the dishwashing detergent bottle. His eye was swollen and red. I overheard him telling momma that he told the people on his job he tripped over one of our toys. The fighting went on for years. He would ruin our Friday family nights. Unbeknown to Daddy, Momma had an escape plan. As soon as our youngest brother, Casey, would become old enough to go to school, we would leave.

It was 1972 and the beginning of integration of schools. Before integration, the schools were segregated. Blacks and whites were now allowed to go to the same schools. Years before, parents were able to choose the neighborhood schools their children attended and it kept the schools segregated. During that time, there was much rivalry between two high schools in downtown Newport News: Collis P. Huntington High School (The Vikings) and George Washington Carver High School (The Trojans). The people who attended those schools had so much school pride. Some of the Huntington Alumni loved to tell stories of the band practicing for the football games. The instruments could be heard throughout the neighborhood and children would watch the band practice as well as march with the band. Because of integration I had to attend Palmer Elementary School, which was at least a 30 minute ride from home. It didn't bother me to be around white students, but I remember everyone looking at each other to see what was different and what was the same.

Momma kept her word. Days after enrolling Casey in kindergarten, we left 406 Maple Avenue and moved to a little, raggedy house, one block from where we lived. It was owned by a man named Mr. Popjack. It was a two-story house that was in disrepair. Looking at it from the front, the house looked like it was leaning to the right side. The house reminded me of the straw house in the story "The Three Little Pigs." It looked as if you could huff and puff and blow it down. It was barely standing alone. When we went to the bathroom, which was downstairs, there was water leaking from the ceiling. I always kept the door open when I used the bathroom because I was afraid. I wondered how long would we have to stay there? Living there was like something out of a scary movie, similar to the ones we used to watch with the spooky voice of Vincent Price or Shelley Winters. The floors made creeping sounds when anyone walked around upstairs. You could hear the water slowly drip, even when no one was in the bathroom. The house was much smaller than what we were used to; it only had two small, dingy bedrooms. However, there was a bright side. Most kids would be upset if their parents separated, but I was so happy that we finally had a life without daddy. There would be no more fighting my momma. Peace in the Valley!

One day as I was getting off of the bus with my sister, I saw momma and Diane outside the front door smiling. I couldn't wait to get to them to find out what was going on. They were ecstatic because momma had received notice from the local housing authority that we qualified for an apartment that was available. We were glad to pack up and move to 677 12th Street in Ridley Circle Apartments, a public housing apartment, where we lived for years to come.

I was in the 4th grade when we moved. Brenda and I had to change from Palmer Elementary to Hidenwood. When I transferred I was placed in a lower level reading class. At Palmer, I was in a 12th grade reading level class because I was very smart and loved to read. When I got to Hidenwood, the highest available level was the 11th grade reading level, and they placed me in that class. I was young, but I remember being called to the office about my new schedule. Those white teachers looked at me as if I were some type of species rather than a smart student. It was as if they didn't know what to do with me because of my high reading capacity. If I were as outspoken then as I am now, I would have said, "It's okay; I'm just a black student who is good at reading."

It was hard on us when momma first left daddy. Financially it was a strain because momma wasn't making much money cleaning houses.

"Lord, I can't believe that's all of the child support they are making Joe give me. I have to figure out something," as she looked at all of us while shaking her head. The child support wasn't enough to cover the bills.

I would always listen to what momma would talk about when she was on the phone. Back then we had the large rotary dial AT&T phones which would sound off loudly as each number was dialed. One day, she called around to find out about public assistance and food stamps. Someone at the Social Services office instructed her to come to a two-story brick building on 25th Street and Wickham Avenue to apply for assistance. We walked with my mom over there because we didn't have a vehicle and it was close enough that we

catch a bus. Upon arrival, the receptionist took some
ttion and had momma fill out some forms.

.hen said, "Mrs. Vick, an eligibility worker will be right
with you."

"Thank you," Mom replied.

You could tell by the look on momma's face, she didn't
want to be in there. Momma wasn't used to any type of assistance.
She and her siblings grew up with a good father who provided for
the family. They called Granddaddy Sam, "Pa." They were used to
having the necessities of life. We waited for about an hour.

"Mrs. Vick, you can come right this way." the receptionist
asked. "This is Mrs. Eaton, your eligibility worker."

"Hello Mrs. Vick, how are you doing?" Mrs. Eaton asked.

Mrs. Eaton was a small, light skinned woman with the
funniest looking mushroom hair style I had ever seen. She was
dressed neatly in a business pants suit. My mom sat down and we
all stood around her.

"Well Mrs. Vick, based on the information you have given
us, it seems you are ineligible for food stamps at this time," Mrs.
Eaton told Momma.

My momma put her head in her hands and paused for a
few minutes. She then raised her head and looked at Mrs. Eaton,
and stated firmly, "Well, if I can't get no food stamps to feed my
children, ya'll gonna have to take my children."

Mrs. Eaton looked at all of us. I guess we were looking real
hungry because the next thing we knew, she was walking over to
momma to tell her we were eligible for the food stamps. Tears came
to my mother's eyes because she was glad to be able to take care of
her children. Mrs. Eaton gave my momma a small card, had her sign
a few documents and we were free to leave.

One thing Momma always said about her marriage union with Joe Vick was "God blessed me with some beautiful children from this one man." She would always remind us that she wanted us, in her terms, "plump" because she did not want anybody thinking we were mal-nourished. Because of all of the outside activity, we were not excessively over weight.

I will never forget when I was in the fifth grade and momma took me to my doctor's appointment. The doctor discussed me being overweight as Momma and I both listened. He gave Momma a prescription and apparently, she was not sure why. Looking back, I don't think he had explained it correctly.

Momma got the prescription filled. It was pills that I had to take before each meal. I came home from school one day and told momma that after taking the pill, I could not eat all of my lunch at school. She got so mad and told me I needed to stop taking the pill. Momma loved us just the way we were, and even though I could not appreciate it at that time, it did wonders for my self-esteem.

My momma did not want us to be too skinny and she made sure we knew that. When we went to school and saw the other children, we thought something was wrong with some of the skinny children and that we were normal sized people. Because all of us were heavily endowed in all of the right places, and momma called us her pretty brown skinned, plump children, we knew we were special. She would often talk about how she was glad she had all of her children by the same man, because she did not want to have a lot of "mix-matched" children. When momma said that, she was referring to women who had children and all of the fathers were different. That was one of the things she didn't tolerate, and she was not afraid to make it clear to all of us.

Spending time outside became a large part of our lives with our Mother as we grew up in Newport News. When transportation was available, we enjoyed trips to parks and occasionally Buckroe Beach in Hampton, but mostly we spent our time outside in our neighborhood. Ridley Circle Apartments in downtown Newport

News was where you could find the Vicks from sun-up to sun-down through our childhood. Somebody was always outside running around imaginary bases for baseball, jumping rope, throwing footballs and bouncing basketballs. Throughout the years, most of the Vicks made an athletic contribution to the "Vicks Got Talent" showcase on the sidewalks of the street we lived on, Ridley Circle.

During the summer, Brenda, Casey and I would walk to the Magruder Pool, which was on 17th Street and Chestnut Avenue. Magruder was a public pool for all of the people in the area. It was about six blocks away from our house, but the walk was worth being able to jump in the cool water.

"Tina, I bet I can beat you to the other side of the pool," Casey challenged.
"I betcha you can't," I said.
"Let's see who can swim the fastest," he said.
"It's on, ready, set, go!" I said.

Casey beat me to our imaginary finish line, because he could swim faster than I. We had each taught ourselves to swim from going to the pool almost every day.

Diane was very good at volleyball so we could always count on her willingness to give us a training session on how to swing your hand back with a strong fist to serve the volleyball over the net—or in our case—over the clothesline. Diane was also good at twirling a baton. Even though we didn't own one, we loved to twirl. We would find old sticks or broomsticks and twirl and march around the sidewalk in the middle of the neighborhood.

Cheering in junior high school was my passion. I just loved to clap and shout and I can remember having a fit if my arms were not straight enough when I performed my cheers. My friend Gwenevere Andrews and I used to practice in our backyard, doing splits, cart wheels, jumps, and all of the arm movements. We were in intermediate school, in 9th grade, when we prepared to try out to be on the Homer L. Ferguson High School (FHS) Cheerleading squad, which was the high school we would be attending the following year.

It was a Thursday evening when we rode the big yellow bus to try out in front of Betsey Redman and her team of judges. We tried to perfect our cheers, which meant having excellent tone coupled with the right amount of volume. Each contestant had ten minutes to convince the judges that we had what it took to be on the FHS cheerleading team. Perform two cheers, demonstrate several jumps and complete a cartwheel and split while smiling were the requirements. The next day, I was ecstatic to see I made the team! I was able to master the art of cheering and became the first one in our family to get selected to such a team.

Once I was a part of the team, I practiced hard and was on time for rehearsals and games. I cheered so hard for that school that you would have thought they were cutting me a weekly check. To this day, I have taught my daughter, family members and close friends' daughters the art of cheerleading.

Casey also worked hard, played very well and made the football team at FHS. He loved football and practiced hard every day. He knew he had to have good grades to continue to play football. There was one coach who had a big influence on Casey's life— Coach Teddy BaCote. His presence in my brother's life couldn't have come at a better time. Because Casey was the baby, the family was very protective of him. We did not want Casey to get hurt on the football field.

When their team had to play Hampton High School (The Crabbers) Casey came home and told us how dangerous it could be because the team was very tough. Well, after the conversation with Casey, momma got scared and figured she should write a note to Coach BaCote to tell him Casey was not feeling well. (She would write a note for everything.) Casey gave the note to Coach BaCote that night before the game. Coach already knew our family well, and he knew we were always babying Casey. He read the note and looked at Casey. I guess he could tell he was not sick and made him get out on the field.

"Get out there, Casey!" he said with his demanding voice.

Casey ended up playing in the game, and we were extremely nervous. Coach could tell we were being over protective. Nothing happened to Casey that night, and we credit Coach BaCote for helping my brother stand up, be a man and face challenges. I'm glad he did because Casey continued to have a relationship with Coach and he became a successful businessman, who owns his own painting company, Vick's Painting and Power Washing. He also has his general contractor's license and is successful in building homes.

Momma always encouraged us to exercise. However, she did not encourage us to make healthy food choices. Several times a day, we would take breaks from running around to visit our local corner stores for refreshments. Two particular stores we frequented were on Ivy Avenue on the corners of 12th and 9th Streets. Kid Chocolate's Store and Taylor's had the best snacks! We would walk to the store and buy candy, sugary treats, drinks, cookies, etc . . . It was nothing for us to hit the pavement two or three times a day for those two cent snacks. And Taylor's Store had the best hamburgers too. They were called "Double D's." We would lean over the counter to watch Mr. Taylor prepare our burger. What made the burgers extra tasty was the way he buttered the bun on the grill first, then added the meat. We would hurry home to eat our burgers.

We always used food stamps when we went to the stores. In those days, it was not the electronic card as it is now, they were paper food stamps. The food stamps were in booklets of different denominations, just like money. I hated going to the store with those foods stamps. The stores downtown wouldn't give any change back. Instead, they would give you what was called a due bill. The due bill was a piece of paper which showed the amount you had left to spend under one dollar. Sometimes my Mom sent us to the store to buy something with a due bill and I just hated it. We would wander from aisle to aisle until everything added up to the amount of due bill. Lord, it felt like everyone in the store knew we were on food stamps. I decided I wasn't gonna live like that when I got older.

Momma was very outspoken when it came to taking care of her business and her family. One day she went to the doctor because she had gotten huge varicose veins. The doctor was concerned the veins would stop my momma's circulation in the future. After the last series of tests, the doctor made his determination. Momma's leg needed to be amputated. Everyone was upset and we were crying. Momma told all of her friends what the doctor said and she asked for their advice.

She finally said, "I am not going to let any doctor take my leg off!"

It's a good thing she didn't because they wanted to take her leg off when she was 37. Momma lived with both of her legs until she died at the age of 76 years old.

We loved being together as a family. We didn't have a lot of rules growing up because momma was a very easy-going mom. She never woke us up at five and six in the morning to scrub baseboards and floors like some of our friends' parents did. Somehow, we just cleaned up and did the right things just because we loved and respected her as our mom.

Joe Jr., Diane and Brenda were the neatest of all of my brothers and sisters. I was always real junky. It didn't and still doesn't take me a long time to mess up an area of the house. I always had lots of books, magazines and other papers on my bed. When I started having homework, I loved to study before I went to bed and I always went to sleep with my books and notebooks around my head. The night before my tests, I slept with whatever material I needed to study under my pillow. I thought that as I slept; the information would sink further into my head. I loved learning, reading, and spelling so much that I would do my homework without being told by mom.

One time momma was being too lenient by allowing us to roller skate in the house on the second floor. Brenda, Casey and I would skate in the hallway. Of course, the wheels rolling on the concrete floors made a loud noise. We also took the top mattress off of the bed and slid down the stairs on the mattress as if it was a sled. One of the neighbors reported us to the rental office and the Housing Authority Officials said we would have to move if we didn't stop. Momma started complaining to her friend Mrs. Lydia, who had about eight children. She complained that the neighbors shouldn't be reporting us to the rental office for skating in the house. The way the apartments were designed on 12th Street, our apartment was in the middle, but our row of attached apartments consisted of eight apartments in total. I guess she thought Mrs. Lydia was going to be on her side, but she told her the neighbors should report us because we should not be skating in the house. Momma couldn't do anything but laugh because she knew Mrs. Lydia was telling the truth. She just wanted her children to be happy.

Over the years, our mornings always began with the same regimen. We would gather in momma's room to talk, listen to the radio, and be in her presence. Momma always turned the radio to WGH and we listened to the voice of Dick Lamb and Daddy Jack Holmes of WPCE. I will never forget how Daddy Jack Holmes would shout out in the morning, "It's seven o'clock . . . get up from there!!" We knew it was no more sleeping. It was time to get up and to get ready for school.

Regardless of the location and how much money we had, all of my earliest memories of my childhood home were happy ones. My mom was a strong woman who left my dad after being physically abused and she never looked back. She had no family in Newport News, and she sometimes relied on my dad's Uncle Virgin and his wife, Aunt Catherine. They would sometimes help out when she needed extra food to feed us. Their house was always a nice place to go to be with family. Uncle Virgin would always have either peach or strawberry homemade wine. He would only allow us to have a sip. We thought we were doing something great by being able to taste the "adult" drink. He was proud about the fact he could make homemade wine. You could tell by the way he described the process he used to make the wine. As he sampled his creation, he would display a boastful grin. It was a treat to go in Aunt Catherine's bedroom to see all of her nail polishes. She would have about 20 bottles. We had never seen anyone with that much nail polish: bright reds, oranges and burgundy. When she polished our nails, we were delighted.

Our life was good, thanks to the strength and love from my wonderful mother. She was the type of mom who loved us for just being her cute, little brown children.

CHAPTER TWO

THE VICK FAMILY

Brenda and Tina in Ferguson cheerleader uniforms

We shared many family stories and loved to laugh and have a good time. Brenda, Casey and I would always tease each other. Momma didn't like the teasing each other. They loved to tease me about having a lot of cavities. Momma spent many days and hours taking me to the dentist. It took us forever to ride the Pentran bus to the Peninsula Health Center where they offered free dental care. The nurse at Dunbar Elementary School sent momma a note to tell her I needed to see a dentist. I had numerous cavities and on my first visit, momma and I were alarmed because the dentist informed us that if I didn't get these problems corrected, it could eventually lead to brain damage and other health problems. We kept our appointments. We waited in the clinic for hours and the work I had to get done to improve my dental problems was extensive. After everything was completed, we breathed a sigh of relief. I continued to do well in school for years, even getting accepted into the National Junior Honor Society and the National Honor Society. After those inductions, momma used to loved to tell people, "Yeah, the dentist said because of all those cavities, Tina could have some brain damage, but and she ended up being the smartest child I have." All of my brothers and sisters were smart, but no one liked to read and study like I did.

Brenda and Casey still laugh about the time we were walking from Lincoln Park and this crazy—looking boy threatened to put a dead bird on us. Casey and Brenda wouldn't say a word to stop him, but I pleaded with the guy not to put that bird on us. He didn't. They teased me about pleading with him to leave us alone.

"Mister don't put that bird on us please, please," I begged. To this day, those two will not let that story die.

Momma use to always dress Brenda and I alike. Even if we didn't have the exact same dress and pants suits, they would be the same color. Sometimes she would buy us the same outfit, but I would have blue and Brenda would have green or vice versa. Once for the winter she brought us matching corduroy coats. The only difference was my coat was gold and Brenda's was burgundy. Everybody thought we were twins because we looked alike and we were only a year apart. I was a year older than Brenda because I was born on February 3, 1962 and Brenda was born April 26, 1963.

The Fourth of July was one of our favorite holidays! Momma just loved Independence Day. She would call around early in the morning and tell all of her sisters, "Happy Fourth!" She always planned something exciting for us, usually at the park. Momma would always go to Rose's or Wilkins Credit Store to get us red, white and blue outfits for the 4th of July holiday. If her money was low, she would go to Wilkins because the owner would allow his regular customers to get merchandise and put it on the credit books. Mr. Wilkins knew Momma was a good, loyal customer and he knew when she got her ADC check on the first of the month, she would faithfully come in and pay on her account. ADC, as I later found out stood for "Aid to Dependent Children." and it was financial assistance for single mothers raising their children.

On that day we would pack up everything and each of Momma's six kids would have something in their hands to take to the park, that is Lincoln Park, which was called Pinkett's Beach before it was purchased by the City of Newport News and renamed in 1968 in memory of President Abraham Lincoln. The Park was on 6th Street and Jefferson Avenue. It was beautiful and comprised of almost 20 acres of land. The rear of the park and its pier entrenched into the Hampton Roads harbor. We lived on 12th Street, so it was a quick six block walk to our destination.

We used to go over our check list over and over, before we left home because we didn't want to leave anything.

"Do we have the aluminum foil?" Momma asked. "What about the cooler with the ice and water?" she asked.
Joe Jr. said, "I got it Ma."
"Ma I got the blanket!" Casey screamed.

Even though there were park tables, we always took a blanket to lie on. After everything was prepared, we would leave. Nobody wanted to keep walking back and forth.

We would find a nice spot under a tree and begin our cook out. The summer wind blowing off of the water from the James River was soothing. There were many families at the park providing a great holiday for their children. We would all stand around Momma and hug her real tight and thank her for giving us such a treat for the wonderful holiday. "Thanks Mommy!"

The times we spent at home were memorable. Diane had this crazy thing she would do when she was trying to scare us. It was called a séance. When Momma was at work, she would have all of us sit around the kitchen table and hold hands.

"Everybody close your eyes," she said. Then she would start calling someone from the dead. "George Washington, George Washington, if you can hear me . . . knock three times." She would use a scary, spooky voice.

In a few seconds, we would hear a knock. We would take off running and hide under the beds or in the closets to get away from the ghosts. We later found out that Diane was using her hand or foot, whichever fit best, to hit the wall or the table to make the knocking sound. She was making the sounds not George Washington.

We would always take some time out of our day to read. Before Momma and Daddy separated, Daddy bought us a set of *The World Book Encyclopedia*. All of us loved sitting around in the living room looking at different volumes. There were two "C" volumes, but the "C to Ch" volume had a section with the tales of Christmas. One section included several Christmas carols which we memorized.

"Let's get together and sing!" Casey said.
"Yeah let's start with *O Come, All Ye Faithful*," Diane said.

That was the first song listed under the large, red Christmas title in the book. Diane would usually be the one holding the book and we'd crowd around her to see the words and sing in unison. We'd sing the entire song then clap for each other.

Casey would say, "What's the next song?"

We would sing *Joy to the World* and all of the Christmas songs written in the encyclopedia. Our family got much use out of those books. We took the book out and sang those songs every Christmas. Even when Diane and Lee-Lee moved out to get their own place, we still sang those songs for the holidays.

One other book our family loved was *The Boxcar Children*. I don't remember who checked the book out of the library on West Avenue, but we read the book over and over. I think everyone loved it because those children were poor and having as difficult times as we were and we could identify with them.

It's time for "Soul Train!" I yelled as I turned our Zenith television console to Channel 13. "Let's watch *Soul Train*. Barry White is going to be on the show," I said.

"Yeah, I love me some Barry White!" Diane said.

All of us would dance in the middle of the floor as we snapped our fingers and sang the introduction to one of our favorite shows.

"People all over the world!" "It's the Soooouuuuulll Train!" "Doop! Doop! Doo-doo doo!" we yelled, as we sang the whistle part of the intro.

Yes, it was time to get on board with the hippest trip in America, the *Soul Train* and its dancers. We would get on board with the host extraordinaire, Mr. Don Cornelius.

When the Soul Train line started, two of us would get on each side to make the *Soul Train* line. We would each take turns dancing down the middle aisle imitating the *Soul Train* dancers. One of us would always come down doing a popular dance called the robot, where you had to move the arms and legs in a mechanical motion, just like a robot. What a good time we had watching that show and trying to guess whose name was scrambled, on the *Soul Train* scramble board. Over the years we watched all the black stars, including the crooning Smokey Robinson and Al Green. We could not stop dancing to the music of the Ohio Players, Chaka Kahn and Rufus and my favorite, Harold Melvin and The Blue Notes.

I would sing along "The world won't get no better, if we just let it be, we gotta change it, yeah, just you and me!!!"

When we were not at home having fun, we were finding ways to work to make our lives better. During the summer months, we would go to our rental office on Saturday morning. We were allowed to sign out a rake and a hoe to work on our yard. We kept the grass in our yard trimmed. We also picked up trash and raked the leaves. We had pride in where we lived.

During our teenage years, we were fortunate to have the benefits of a program that provided summer jobs. The Office of Economic Opportunity, or OEO, as the agency was called by folks in the neighborhood sponsored the program. Some people would say the acronyms so fast it sounded like they were saying "OREO". The program was started during the presidential administration of the 36th President, Lyndon B. Johnson, who declared a "War on Poverty," during his term. The federal funds were used to create community action agencies. These agencies were designed to create jobs and job training to allow opportunities for poor people to become self-sufficient. One of the programs was the summer jobs program. The funds were administered through OEO under a Neighborhood Youth Corps grant. OEO provided summer jobs for low income families. The agency provided minimum wage jobs at summer lunch feeding sites, Fort Eustis and Fort Monroe, the Veteran's Administration and recreation centers. These summer jobs allowed young people an opportunity to work and obtain a work ethic. Diane was always good at typing and was able to get a job as a secretarial aid at Fort Monroe. It was a blessing for her to get the job because Momma needed extra money to buy our school clothes. Diane was glad to be able to help because Momma had done so much for us.

It didn't seem fair that Diane had to work and spend her money on us. She didn't seem to mind because she was a good big sister and she always looked out for us. She learned how to type and take shorthand. She told all of us to learn how to type and answer a phone professionally, and we would always be able to keep a job. For many years after she told us this, my goal was to be a secretary because I loved the typewriter. Each summer we looked forward to applying for the summer jobs and working to make things easier on Momma. I was glad to get my first job, which was a recreation aide at Lincoln Park, one of the recreation sites. I was 14 years old. Every day we did arts and crafts with the children. We made pot holders, beaded bracelets and all kinds of designs with fabrics and glue. I was glad to get my first check and even happier to get my second, third and fourth checks. It made it more clear to me that people don't have to live month to month on one check like we did living on the welfare system. I liked the idea of being able to get out and work and make my own money. I worked hard every day and was glad the OEO gave opportunities for people to have a better life. With one of my checks I was able to buy my first yellow ten speed bike. I used my bike as my transportation to and from my job.

After the work week, on Friday afternoons, we would sit on the front porch. Many of our neighbors would walk past our apartment and have conversations with us. Momma was a good listener and people loved talking to her about their problems. You would have thought she had a written sign on her door which read: "Office of Psychologist Caletha Vick." Momma would come home from cleaning white peoples' houses and complain about all of the people she saw on the Pentran bus who wanted to talk to her about their problems.

"Lord, I am glad to get home," she would exclaim, "I can't believe people have so many problems with their lives." She just couldn't believe the people who would come to her with all of their problems. "Lord I just can't believe these people are talking to me about all of these problems," she would say, "What in the world? People want to talk to me about everything that is challenging them in their lives." she would say. "I wish I did have all of the answers."

At home, we always talked loudly. When the entire family was together, our neighbors probably thought we were arguing instead of talking. All of us yelled when we talked even though we were within inches of each other.

"Ya'll be quiet; you know the neighbors can hear ya'll," Momma would say when it got too loud. We would be quiet for a minute or two then back to the loudness.

My brother Joe Jr. would come in the house sometimes and think it was an emergency. "Ma what's wrong?" he asked as he held the screen door open, looking puzzled.

"Nothing is wrong with us in here? What are you talking about?" she inquired. She would blare her eyes open and look at us as if to ask, "Is he crazy?

Joe Jr. replied, "Great God! Ya'll in here screaming and talking so loud I thought something bad had happened. I thought somebody was in here fighting."

"You know we been talking loud like this for years, Joe Jr," Diane said, "Plus, you know we got to get our points across," she said laughing.

When we were older, all of us loved sitting at Momma's house during the weekends and for holidays. It was no question where we would meet for the holidays because we knew it would be at Momma's. All of us enjoyed sitting around and talking about old stories of growing up as a Vick.

CHAPTER THREE

A NEW GENERATION

Tina and my neice, Christina Nicole Vick (Niki)

Aunt Tina playing w/Michael Vick (9 months)
and Christina Vick (3 years)

Picture from left to right—Niki, Marcus, Teunsha,
Felix, Ravin and Courtney

I was sad when my sister had to get off of the cheerleading squad because our sponsors noticed her stomach looked larger than normal in her cheerleading uniform. They told me I needed to ask my momma to take her to the doctor. I hadn't noticed Brenda's stomach. Honestly, when I think back over my life, my whole world was about cheering, studying, and community service. What baffled me was that I didn't notice it even though Brenda and I slept in the same room?

It was a cold winter night during football season when Homer L. Ferguson High School (The Mariners) was playing Warwick High School (The Raiders) for the homecoming game. I loved the homecoming football games. We always wore our beautiful white sweaters with the huge light blue "F" on it, our Ferguson-blue pleated skirts, and our white gloves. We completed our uniform by wearing our long, white socks and black and white saddle oxfords. That particular night our sponsor, Mrs. Hodges, noticed Brenda did very few jumps after the cheers. She made remarks about her uniform looking tight in the stomach area. She told Brenda she could not come back without a doctor's note. Weeks later, the doctor's note confirmed what Mrs. Hodges believed—Brenda was pregnant or "like that" as my momma would say. My momma would never say the word pregnant; she would always say "like that." Brenda had to get off of the cheerleading squad permanently. Most people were comfortable asking me about Brenda's situation instead of her.

My oldest sister, Diane, had already gotten pregnant at the age of fifteen. I knew over time it was hard on my momma and oldest sister when she had Lee-Lee as a teen. It takes a toll on the entire family when young children who are not employed and have not completed their education have an unplanned pregnancy. Back in the seventies when Diane got pregnant, the school system did not allow the girls to continue to go to their high school; they had to go to a special school for pregnant girls. From the examples I had seen in my neighborhood, most girls who got pregnant early had to get on welfare and food stamps. I did not want that for my life. I knew I wanted to have a good education and a good job. I also wanted to be married before I had children.

It was hard on me because I was in all advanced classes and most of the students in those classes just didn't get pregnant in high school. Everyone kept asking me questions about what Brenda and her baby's father, Pickle were going to do about the pregnancy instead of asking Brenda. His real name was Michael Boddie.

"Tina, what is your family going to do about your sister having a baby?" Denise asked me. She was in my biology class and we talked all the time.

"What do you mean, what are we gonna do?" I asked her back.

"That's a lot, with her having a baby at such a young age," Denise said.

"I know it is, but that is my sister and our family will work this out so she can keep going to school," I said. "We'll make it through."

Brenda ended up having two children before she finished school. She was still living with Momma in Ridley Circle Apartments and two months before I left for college, she had Michael.

My sister Brenda was a good young Mother and spent a lot of time with her children. Her oldest child, Christina (Niki) was always dressed in the best of clothes. Niki was a beautiful, chocolate little girl. Brenda would always comb her curly, black hair into the most flattering hairstyles with colorful ribbons and barrettes. Brenda often worried about having her skirts and shirts matching. She always had Niki in the cutest little baby doll dresses and all styles of black patent leather dress shoes. In fact, Niki had more dress shoes than toddler walking shoes or sneakers. When she entered the First Step program in Newport News Public schools at age four, it became an issue. The teacher actually requested that Brenda dress Niki in some sneakers because she was sliding around in the shoes in physical education class.

I used to teach Niki all kinds of cheers and we used to create dance routines off of different songs. Our favorite routine was the one we made to the song by Jocelyn Brown, "Can't get off of my horse, and I can't let go." The title was "Somebody Else's Guy." We had a routine for the entire song. Niki had another special song which I loved. It was the song she loved and continued to practice, "I'm Not Your Superwoman," by Karyn White. Niki would put her "little" nose in the air as she created a microphone with her hand and started singing. It was delightful to see her confidence. When she sang it, she owned the lyrics.

I had been successful in high school and continued to learn the skills for success. I knew it was important to be able to communicate with people as well as speak in front of groups without being shy. I knew it would build Niki's confidence if she became accustomed to performing and cheering with confidence. I knew from my success, if you are not afraid to speak and perform in front of people, you could do anything. I wanted to prepare her early for success.

Niki was always a great child in school and the sweetest child at home. Everybody loved her and she especially loved her family. She was a Grandma's child. When she started her first year in school, my mother just couldn't accept her being away from home. If Niki complained about anything before she left for school that morning, or seemed increasingly irritable the night before, Momma would tell Brenda to let Niki stay at home. Her years spent in "First Step" were just that–"a first step"–and Momma did not like that at all. She somehow believed that our home was a safe haven, and if anyone tried to bother us or if there were any unfavorable situations outside, she knew her home was the place to be. At year's end, Niki had been absent at least 91 days of her first year in public school.

By the time Michael began his first year in school, Momma had relaxed a little. Michael attended class regularly and it did not take long before everyone realized he would be a very good student. He listened to the teachers and quickly became a leader in the classroom. He was a handsome young student. As Michael progressed through Hidenwood Elementary School, he continued to excel. Discipline occurrences were rare; however, like many other young boys, he would occasionally push his limits. One day in particular, he had been so disruptive in class that my sister got a call from the school. The principal, Mr. White, had Michael in the office and requested that my sister Brenda come to the office to discuss his behavior.

My sister began to panic as soon as she hung up the phone. I tried to keep her calm. With the exception of Joe Jr. years earlier, the Vick children did not have any problems in school, except for Lee Lee, who didn't want to do any work. We had all loved and spoiled him. We loved having Lee Lee around. Our family related discipline problems with unruliness and we all knew from previous experiences with Joe Jr. that a phone call indicated a red flag. We discussed the experiences that Momma had gone through with Joe Jr., dropping out of high school; going in and out of jails; having to deal with a bail bondsman; and being locked up for his birthdays and holidays. We honestly didn't want life to end up like that for anyone else.

I remember that day vividly; I can even recall my thoughts during that meeting as I glanced around the room at each person. Brenda was seven months pregnant with Marcus at the time, and she remained standing during the meeting. I knew my sister well, and I noticed as soon as the principal began talking that she would not make it through the meeting without crying. I could tell she was hurt, worried and upset.

When I looked at Michael, I knew he had realized that he acted inappropriately. I could tell he was remorseful as he sat motionless, looking at the floor. For the first time, I then thought about my appearance. I glanced down at my outfit when I realized I had left out of the house in such a hurry I still had a scarf tied around my head. I wondered to myself what the principal may have been thinking of the Vick Family as we assembled in his office. My concern for my nephew, far outweighed what I looked like at that time.

Mr. White began to discuss Michael's behavior during the course of the day. He explained to us that his fourth grade teacher noticed Michael was behaving completely out of character. He began interrupting her lesson plans by speaking out of turn, and holding conversations with other students while the teacher was talking. After a couple of verbal warnings, he continued to disturb the class to the point she could no longer tolerate it. Mr. White felt it was necessary to ask Brenda to come to the school to understand that although this was only a verbal warning, if something like this were to happen again, Michael would face steeper penalties.

First, my sister thanked Mr. White for the opportunity to correct the situation before it got out of hand. Then she assured him that this would be the last time he saw Michael in his office. After that, she directed her conversation to her son, and as he began to cry, she told Michael, "You KNOW—you know better than to act like this!" I continued the conversation reminding him that the wrong crowd will get him in trouble, and not just in school, but with the law. Soon both my sister and I were in the office crying and sobbing and scolding Michael, all at the same time.

Although the meeting started out calm and composed, it practically turned into a healing and deliverance service before it was over! I am certain Mr. White did not know what was going to happen next. As he sat there calmly during our emotional time, we spoke to Michael's behavior between sobs. "I want you on the right path!" Brenda told him. I believe at one point Mr. White expected us to start laying hands on Michael and throwing anointing oil on his forehead. Brenda and I thanked him and left his office with tears still in our eyes. After that meeting, Brenda had no more problems with Michael in school.

For years I felt Mr. White must have thought we were crazy. To this day, every time I run into him, I apologize for what I call our "emotions in overkill" on that day. Each time I saw him, he would respond with a chuckle and say, "Don't worry about it; I know you all just wanted what was best for Michael; I understand." I have always thought Mr. White was able to read inside our hearts. He knew exactly how many young boys found themselves heading down a negative path in Newport News, especially downtown where we grew up. Many young boys veered in the direction of standing on the street corners, peddling drugs, stealing vehicles, robbing people and eventually landing their place in prison. No, that would not be the life for my children or my nieces and nephews. No one else in the Vick Family would end up in jail.

One weekend I could not wait to get home to see family. I tried to get home at least once a month to be with my family since I was only in Richmond, Virginia. I always kept my key to our house. It was a Friday afternoon when I arrived.

"Hey Tina!" Momma said as we gave each other a big hug. "What a good surprise today."

"I'm glad to see you Ma," I said. "We have loads of work in college and much more reading than high school."

"I know it is." she said. "I don't know how you read all of those books with no pictures in them." Momma said shaking her head as she laughed. My family teased me for years for reading books with no pictures in them. They thought it was absurd for anyone to read a book and not see any pictures.

"Hey Tina!" Brenda yelled.

"Brenda, hey. I know you love having our room to yourself!" I laughed.

"Yes I sure do, and now when you come home I can tell you to go to "chair," Brenda said laughing. When I came home on the weekends, she had a joke about telling me to sleep on the sofa instead of the bed in our room.

"Where are Niki and Oogie?" I asked. "Shhh, they are upstairs asleep and don't talk too loud, because I know they will be up in a little while," Brenda whispered.

"I know those little rascals won't sleep long," I said. "I should go and wake them up."

"You better not try to wake them up Tina; they will be up soon enough," Brenda said.

"Good, because I have a surprise for them," I said.

"What is it?" Brenda asked.

"It's a surprise and I will tell you when they wake up," I said. "Um, Momma what are you cooking? It smells delicious?" I asked.

"Just some Rice-A-Roni with some hamburgers in it," she said. I don't know why we called everything with ground beef in it hamburgers, but Momma sure knew how to make some good Rice-A-Roni. I think it was extra good because she left some of the grease from the ground beef in the pan before she put the rice in it, which made an extra special flavor. Momma prepared both Brenda and I a plate.

"This Rice-A-Roni is so good Momma," I said.

"Thanks, it's just a meal I threw together," Momma said laughing.

"I wish we had this meal at school," I added. We sat at the table and talked and laughed.

Then we heard the pitter-patter of some small feet coming down the stairs. I jumped up and hid in the closet in the kitchen. They came downstairs and Niki got in Momma's lap and Oogie sat in the chair beside Brenda.

"Surprise!" I screamed as I jumped out of the closet.

"Aunt Tina!!" they both screamed and we all hugged each other. They loved when I came home from college because we just loved spending time together.

"I got a surprise for ya'll," I said.

"What is it?" they both asked.

"This evening we are going to Peter Piper Pizza and then we are going to see a play at my old high school."

"Yes, I love Peter Piper Pizza." Oogie said.

"We will leave about 5 o'clock because the play starts at 7 o'clock," I said. "It will give us a chance to have dinner then go to see *Oklahoma*. It's just going to be me and both of you. Your Momma is not going, so don't be crying," I told them.

Brenda was with them all of the time and they just loved her. We sat outside on the porch and watched them play outside. Momma and I talked some more. Five o'clock came and we walked to the parking lot to get in the car. Brenda always had them looking their best.

"Are you ready to go?" I asked. "Yeah, Aunt Tina," they said. Brenda dressed Niki in the cutest little blue cotton dress with matching hair bows. Oogie had on khakis and his lumber jack shirt and the cutest dress shoes.

I put my niece and nephew in the seat belts and we pulled out of the parking lot. They kept looking back at Brenda waving until she was no longer in sight. They asked me questions all the way to Peter Piper Pizza, which was approximately a fifteen minute drive. We ate our pepperoni pizza and headed across the street to Ferguson High School to see the play, *Oklahoma*.They enjoyed the play for a while, but when it lasted a little too long, both of them kept squirming in their seats.

"I'm ready to go Aunt Tina," Oogie said.

"Hold on just a little bit, the play will be over soon," I told him.

After the play was over, we headed home. We had a joyous evening and I was happy to be with them because I loved being with my niece and nephew.

In 1983, Marcus was born. By this time all of Momma's children had graduated from high school and moved out. In the apartment on 12th Street, it was only Momma, Brenda and her children. A few years after Marcus was born, Brenda ended up getting an apartment in Newport News on Lassiter Drive. During that time, if a child lived in public housing and graduated from high school and wanted to continue to live at home, the public housing manager would not allow the child to stay on the lease. If you got a job and wanted to continue to live with your parents, they would factor your income into how much rent you had to pay and it was usually so expensive that you may as well move to a market rate apartment. What ended up happening was many young people from public housing didn't get a chance to have some money saved before they found another place to live. Neither did our parents have any money saved to give us for a healthy start to adult life. Since all of us were gone and Brenda had moved, the housing authority moved Momma to a one bedroom place on Lassiter Drive which was about a half a block away from Brenda's apartment. God really worked that out because Momma was close enough to continue to help Brenda with her children.

Marcus was the sweetest little boy. As he grew older, he sucked his thumb. He would look at you with those big, innocent eyes. As his aunt, when I would look at his eyes and that big head I would do whatever he asked me to do. One time, I volunteered to keep Marcus when I came home for winter break from college. Marcus and I had returned from the store. When I came in our house I realized I didn't get his bottle out of the car. I sat Marcus on the living room sofa and went back to the car. It didn't register in my head to take him with me. When I came back, Marcus had leaped up and then he fell off of the sofa and onto the floor. He was crying when I came back in the house and I was upset. His little lips were swollen and I could not hold him tight enough!! "Oh my goodness! Oh my Marcus," I screamed as I held him tight to my chest, "Oh

Aunt Tina's baby, I am so, so sorry!" as Marcus continued to cry. "Brenda is going to kill me when she finds out I let you fall on this floor," I said to him even though he wasn't old enough to know what I was talking about. "Aunt Tina is sorry she let this happen to you, but it's gone be alright," I said. Even though I said this, I was scared because Brenda was very protective of her children and she never let anyone keep them except for family members. I had allowed this to happen to her third born. I had the hardest time explaining to her what had happened because I felt badly. She trusted me with her child and I allowed him to fall off of the sofa. To this day, Marcus claims I threw him out of the car.

CHAPTER FOUR

LIFE ON MY OWN

When I graduated from Homer L. Ferguson High School in 1980, I had a plan in place for my life. Although I was not ecstatic about leaving my family and friends in Newport News, I knew it was a must if I wanted to better my quality of life. My goal was to find a good job, not only to make money, but to have a job with a good title. The federal survey cards we had in the public schools really affected me. They were the small cards given to the students on the first day of school designed to give the federal government information about our parents. Information included where they worked and how many people were in the family. We were required to turn them in to our teachers the first week of school. Since I was smart, I was in classes with mostly white students. They would look at each others' cards comparing what each parent did to make a living. Most of their parents were either directors, coordinators, in the military or had a good, high-paying job. I would hide my card until the teacher called to collect it because I hated having the word "welfare" written on my federal survey card for my Mother's job.

I was extremely embarrassed by the situation. I felt that if I was asked by my peers to explain "welfare," I wouldn't want to explain it. I was very quiet on the day that the teacher collected the survey cards. I kept my card in my book bag until the teacher called for all of the cards. I thought to myself at an early age that I wanted to have a good job, so that when I had children, they would be proud of my place of employment as well as my position. I never wanted them to feel the embarrassment that I felt.

I was accepted in the only two universities where I had applied, Virginia Commonwealth University (VCU) and the University of Richmond. Looking at real dollars and cents, I knew I needed to attend VCU because the cost of the education was much less. At that time, VCU's tuition, including room and board, was only approximately $3,000 a year. The tuition at the University of Richmond was double that amount. Also, VCU had an excellent communications department and I was very interested in being a news broadcaster. The students were afforded an opportunity to work for VCU's radio and television program. When I visited the campus, I was pleased to see all nationalities of people on the university's campus, even though it was a predominately white university at that time.

Leaving home was such a sad day. I wanted to further my education, but leaving my family was very difficult. I was the first one to leave our home to attend a four year college. I was proud to be the first one to venture off to further my education. My mom and siblings along with my nieces and nephews, were all gathered on the porch of our home at 12th Street to say our good-byes. We waited for Joe Jr.'s girlfriend, Shawnda Futrell, to take me to Richmond, Virginia, because, when I left for college, we still didn't have a car. All of us were crying and Lee-Lee cried the worst. His loud burst of tears made us all think we were attending a funeral. His crying made everybody feel really bad. Before Shawnda and I took off, my mom put $20.00 in my hand and we hugged each other tightly.

"Love ya, love ya," Momma said.
"I love you too, Momma!!"

Then Shawnda and I pulled off in her white Monte Carlo and it was off to my life on my own.

Shawnda Futrell not only loved my brother, but she loved our entire family. She was very pretty, with beautiful vanilla skin and dark brown hair. Her hair was cut very short and tapered in the back. She was from the Phoebus area of Hampton, Virginia. She dressed in the best clothes and compared herself to the actress Alexis Carrington from the television show, *Dynasty*.

College life was an unforgettable experience. Even though I only had $20.00 in my pocket, I had the determination of a millionaire. I enjoyed the college atmosphere. For the very first time, I was exposed to different cultures, traditions, and even diverse lifestyles. I loved the big City of Richmond and being there made me feel free.

Of course, I was looking for the opportunity to become a cheerleader in college, but when I got to VCU, and saw their cheerleaders with those teeny weeny legs, I knew they were not going to choose me. I was a size 13 and my thighs looked like chocolate ham hocks compared to those girls. I wasn't about to starve and loose all that weight just to be thrown in the air, which could lead to me plunging to my death. Since I was majoring in communications and wanted to be a news reporter, I joined the campus radio station as an announcer and disc jockey.

During my time in school, the singer Luther Vandross was very popular and I was mesmerized by his melodic voice. The station manager had to talk to me about diversifying my music because I would dedicate an entire hour to playing Luther Vandross songs on the campus radio station. Even though I wanted to listen to "Luther" all night, that didn't mean other people wanted to listen to him. The station manager continued to encourage me to play a variety of music. He was very fond of my DJ name, "Tasmania Tina."

Many of my friends were not accepted into VCU because of their poor grades and low SAT scores. I was accepted and received a scholarship to attend. The Pell grants that I qualified for helped me to pay for my first year. While in high school, I had been an excellent student. I was inducted into the National Honor Society and was also a member of the Varsity Cheerleaders, Keyettes, *The Windjammer* newspaper and the Yearbook staff. I was also involved in a community organization, the Youth Advisory Board (YAB). Mr. Ben Timmons recruited me and a lot of other teenagers who lived in public housing to join the board. Our job was to attend monthly meetings and become a governing body for activities for youth.

Our advisor was a man from South Carolina, Mr. Robert D. Ayers, Jr. who allowed us to call him "Bob." We planned Easter Egg hunts for the neighborhood, youth dances, and talent shows. We also bought a soda machine for the Lassiter Courts Recreation Center and put the drinks in the machine. All of the money we made went into our non-profit account. We saved enough money to give all of the members a $50.00 gift when they graduated from high school.

Bob and his wife, Martha were the nicest people. He had migrated here because of the military and when he retired, he stayed in the area. He would excite us with his stories of the South Carolina State Bulldogs and the distinguished men of Kappa Alpha Psi Fraternity, Incorporated. In fact, I didn't really want to go to college at first. I wanted to just get a job at this Burger King that was on 30th Street and Jefferson Avenue and work my way up to be the manager. I figured with a manager's salary, I would get enough money to get a car. I was tired of our family walking, catching buses, or waiting for people to come and pick us up.

When I was 17, I had gotten a summer job as a secretarial aide. I wanted to see if I could save some money to buy a car. I had taken my driver's education course, passed the driver's range with the infamous Dick Tyson and passed the test to get my license. Passing that test was hard for me, but I wanted to get it done. I remember the final day of taking the class on the range at Todd's Stadium. We did the skid testing and we stayed longer than our regular two hours. The last city bus came at 7 pm. He finally gave me my paperwork and I headed to the bus stop to catch the last bus.

It was already time for the last bus for Ivy Avenue. It was freezing cold, as I walked across the field. There was snow on the ground from a snow storm earlier that week. I saw the bus coming, but I wasn't close to the bus stop. I started running in the wedged-heeled boots, screaming to the top of my lungs, "BUS! BUS!" I was trying to get the bus to stop. The bus driver didn't hear me and kept going. I found myself walking all the way down to the east end to make it home. I didn't have anyone to call for a ride.

I started walking and made it close to Ferguson High School at the nearby Lou Smith's grocery store.

A guy named Ron saw me and asked me, "Where I was going?"

I told him, "I had missed the last bus and did not have a way home."

He told me, "Get in the car." Since he lived in Newsome Park, he would give me a ride home.

I was thankful I didn't have to walk to the other end of town in the cold. We had a quiet ride home to 12th Street.

Since I had passed the range test, I went to Department of Motor Vehicles (DMV) to get my license. When I drove up to the window of DMV, the tester was very mean. His words were, "You barely passed it!" I took the card he gave me and said, "Thank you." I was nervous as hell. Once I got my license, I kept a good driving record.

On pay day I got my check of $317.00. I wanted to buy me some kind of car. I was just sick of us not having a car, so I was going to figure out how to get one. I finished my work day and got on the Pentran bus to go home. As I rode past a car dealership, I saw a powder-blue Pinto for $100.00. "Oh my God!!! I have got to call Mr. Bob Ayers to go with me to check out this car!" I mumbled to myself. "One hundred dollars, I can afford that," I thought to myself. I got off the bus at my normal stop on 12th Street and Ivy Avenue. I ran home to call Bob.

"Hello Martha, how are you doing?" I asked when she answered the phone.

"I'm fine dear," Martha said as she was always pleasant on the phone.

"Is Bob at home?"

"Oh yes he is, let me get him for you, sweetie," Martha replied.

"Hello, Bob Ayers," Bob said as he got the phone from Martha.

"Bob, you are not going to believe this! I found a car, a powder-blue Pinto for $100.00!" I told him with much excitement.

"Humm, one hundred dollars?" he pondered.

"Yes, yes, I saw it today when the bus rode pass the car place," I said.

"I would have to go and see that for one hundred dollars because that is a very low price for a car," he said.

"It's there, it's on the lot and the price is $100.00. Can you please take me there tomorrow to check it out?"

"Let me see, let me see what time I'm available tomorrow," he said.

"Well, I have to work until 4 pm," I explained to Bob.

"How about 5:30?" he asked.

"Yes, I can be ready?" I said. "Can you pick me up from my house?" I asked.

"Yes indeed, yes, yes I can," said Bob.

Bob picked me up the next day and I couldn't wait to get to the car dealership. I had waited with much anticipation all day and it was now time to go and get my car!! I had my money and I was ready. We got out of the car and I pointed to the powder-blue Pinto.

"There it is! There it is!" I pointed.

Bob walked around to the front of the car to see the price. "Oh no Tina, this is one thousand dollars," he said, They have the other zero over in the corner."

My heart was crushed. I thought I was close to my dream of getting a vehicle, but that was the company's marketing tactic to lure potential buyers to their dealership. The fourth zero was small and written in the very corner of the window, which made it look like a hundred dollars instead of a thousand.

"Well Tina, Bob said, It's going to happen. You will be able to get your car sooner or later."

"I know I will Bob," I said in a discouraged tone. "But I wanted it to be sooner rather than later."

After volunteering with Bob and realizing how college can make an individual's life better, I decided to go. I was very serious about my studies and didn't hang around anyone who wasn't serious about college. If I met a student who had been in college for three years or more and was still a freshman, I would not have them in my circle. I planned to finish school on time, because I knew that with a degree, I was going to graduate and land a reporting job making at least $30,000 a year, and life was going to be great!! I had to resist all negative influences.

I remember my first encounter with exercising my ability to say no to drugs in college. One of my friends had a friend who would come to her room and bring her cocaine.

"Tina, girl, you should try this cocaine; it is not bad," Shirley said to me. "All it does is make you feel happy."
"No!" I told Shirley. "I am not about to put that mess up my nose because my nose is too small and it might blow my nose off." That was the end of that ordeal.

It was the end for me because I knew from watching people around my neighborhood that drugs were the beginning of a dead end road. It either landed you in jail or the land of the walking dead. It was disheartening watching a few of the people in my community whose daily lives consisted of purposelessly standing around on the street corners since drugs and alcohol had consumed their lives.

My first semester at VCU, the number of students accepted to attend VCU had superceded the number of dormitory rooms that were available on campus. Instead of being in the dorms, I was housed at the William Byrd Hotel, which was 12 blocks from VCU's main campus. A shuttle came every half hour to pick up students and take us to the campus. It was convenient and gave me more independence. Once I got used to the City of Richmond, I would usually walk to class. Richmond had the longest blocks, unlike the ordinary cities.

My first roommate was an Asian girl named Jessica Shih. She was very nice. I think she was rich because she said her Daddy owned a hospital in Taiwan. We got along very well. We had only one problem. Since we were in the William Byrd Hotel, we had our own bathroom with a shower and bathtub. We had to clean our own room and clean the tub after we used it.

"Jessica, we need to talk. I noticed you don't clean the bathtub after you get out of the shower," I said.

She had a confused look as she replied, "I don't know how to clean bathtub."

"What?" I said, looking just as confused as she did. "You don't know how to clean the tub?"

"In Taiwan, we have maid," she said in her Asian accent, "They clean for us."

"Oh, okay," I said. I was thinking, were there black maids in Taiwan and did she think I fit the bill? Or were there Asian maids? Either way I wanted to let her know that she was in the regular every day world of America now. It was our responsibility to keep the bathroom clean and not just mine. I responded kindly, "Well Jessica, this is not Taiwan, this is America. Come with me in the bathroom and I will show you how to clean this tub." Both of us went into the bathroom. I held the jar of Comet, with a cleaning sponge and showed her how to clean the tub. From then on Jessica and I didn't have any problems.

In the Fall of 1981, I submitted my letter for acceptance to the first black Greek letter sorority, Alpha Kappa Alpha Sorority, Incorporated. Alpha Kappa Alpha sorority was founded in 1908 on the campus of Howard University in Washington, D.C. My Aunt Ethel sent me the $150.00 it cost to pledge and I was thankful for that. Aunt Ethel was the best aunt we had. She was my mother's sister who would come visit us every year from New York. She lived in Brooklyn, and we thought she was exciting and rich because she would always fly to Virginia. Momma would be glad to see her and they would hug each other tightly and just laugh and joke the entire time Aunt Ethel was in Newport News. Momma never traveled and she said it was because one of her older sisters had taken a trip with her boyfriend and they got in a tragic car accident and were killed. From then on she was very cautious about all kinds of travel.

Momma rarely went anywhere, not even to Hampton, Virginia, which was only minutes away.

I went to New York to stay with Aunt Ethel for my summer break from VCU. I had taken the Greyhound bus, which was about a thirteen hour ride with the longest stop in Washington, D.C.

"Hey miss!" the security guard yelled. "Are those your bags!"

I looked back to make sure he was pointing to my bags. "Yes sir, they are mine." I said. "You gotta stay with your bags miss, you have to stay with your bags!" he yelled again. "Sure, I just wanted to find the restroom." I said feeling somewhat intimidated.

"Well, if you going to the bathroom, you gotta take your bags with you! You don't want nobody to get your bags," he stated with his rough, raspy voice.

I turned around and picked up my two bags.

I had my light blue luggage bag that was my pride and joy because that was the bag Mrs. Louise Bazemore had given me from the Ridley Circle Tenant Council. Mrs. Bazemore was a community advocate who held regular meetings at the Ridley Circle Recreation Center. I attended the meetings as a teenager and they were fascinated how involved I was in community service at such a young age. At the last meeting, before it was time for me to leave for Richmond, they presented me with a token of appreciation, which was a piece of luggage. They bid me farewell on my way to college. I definitely didn't want anyone to take that bag because I treasured what they had given me. It signified the beginning of my journey. We stayed in Washington, D.C. for about thirty minutes then it was back to boarding the bus for our destination—The Big Apple!!!

Once I got there, my cousin, James wanted me to help him with his blade sharpening business. He would sharpen small blades on a blade sharpening machine that was attached to a generator inside his minivan. My cousin's rundown off-white minivan and his powerful generator were extremely loud. The entire block could hear the noise when he would crank up his van to sharpen small blades. Together we would ride through the streets of New York in Brooklyn, Harlem and in the Bronx, looking for barbers, as well as pet grooming parlors, that used blades for razors for their respective businesses. The biggest problem was that we would drive all around town for hours and sharpen approximately four blades or sometimes even less, only to earn about $20.00 per day. I could clearly see that this job was a waste of time and not producing enough monies for me. I informed him that I needed to make more money.

In the eighties, there were no online applications; therefore, I had to ask my cousin to take me to a variety of employment agencies and employment temporary services to look for a job. I checked the "help wanted" ads daily to see if there was any job I could apply for. I needed more money than what we could get from sharpening the blades. It just wasn't enough income.

"Hello this is Tina Vick, I applied for the Girl Friday position you had in the classifieds last week."

"Um huh, how can I help you?" asked the receptionist.

"Well, I want to know if the position is still open?" I said.

"I'm sorry, the Girl Friday position has already been filled," she said, "but thank you for calling."

"Thank you," I said as I slowly hung up the phone with disappointment. I was at my Aunt Ethel's house. "Dang, Aunt Ethel, they picked somebody else." I said.

"Oh they did," Aunt Ethel replied.

"Oh man, and I needed the job to make some money for the summer."

"Some other job will come through and it may be better," she told me in an encouraging tone.

She was right! My cousin, Sonny was working as a packer with this small, Mexican spice company, Jane Butel's Pecos River Spice Company. It was in Queens, New York located in Long Island City. He told the owner, Jane Butel about his cousin from Virginia who was here in New York looking for a job. Ms. Butel interviewed me for the assistant to the secretary position and she called me the next day to let me know she was hiring me for the job. Sonny was proud to see me coming to work and not playing around, but working hard and doing my job well.

I earned the position as the administrative assistant, and I helped her run the small office. It was a mail order company. Her secretary and I would open the mail to see what order forms were in the envelopes. The company shipped out authentic Tex-Mex spices all over the United States. I would type up all the orders and then take them to the packing room. My sister Diane had told all of us early on to learn how to type and answer a phone professionally. She believed if you knew how to do those two things, you could always keep a job. I had learned how to type in the ninth grade and now I had a job. I was glad I had taken her advice.

I had great administrative skills and my phone etiquette was perfect. I would walk to the warehouse where the orders were prepared and shipped to give them the list of morning orders. The job paid weekly, which was perfect for me. I did lots of shopping for me and my Aunt Ethel. I learned how to catch the subway train from Brooklyn to Queens, New York, where my job was located. I was proud of myself!! Here I was a southern college student who was able to come to New York, find a job, catch the train and even make it in the BIG APPLE!

One day, I opened the office and went into the warehouse. My desk was located in the front office, and each day I would put my purse in the second desk drawer. My morning routine was to check the phone messages, to open the mail, and to prepare Ms. Butel's coffee. This particular Monday, I went to the warehouse to talk to Sonny and Regaston, our co-worker who was from the West Indies. Regaston was a fine, dark man who had a heavy West Indies accent. He had a strong work ethic and he was impressed with Sonny's and my work ethic.

He said in his West Indies accent, "It is very rare you meet Black Americans like you two who want to work hard."

"Well thank you," Sonny said. "I learned to work hard when I had to farm in the country in North Carolina. We had to pick tobacco, cotton and shuck corn when I was a little boy." Then Sonny laughed and said, "And Tina, I tell you girl, Aunt Red didn't like to work in those fields, yeah, Aunt Red hated working in the fields. Sometime I would look over and she would be lying down in the fields." We all laughed.

Regaston then added, "It is important to work hard here in America, because nobody is going to give you anything," he pointed out.

"Amen to that," I said "I'm sorry gentlemen, I have to go back to my office."

As I headed back to the front office, I turned the corner and saw an older black man, looking somewhat tattered and torn, standing near my desk.

"Can I help you, sir?" I asked. He stood there almost in shock. He could not move. As I was about to ask him again how could I help you, I looked down at his hand and he had my beautiful black purse. "You, you, you got my pocket book!" I screamed. "Give me my pocketbook!" I screamed again.

He looked at me and slowly handed me the purse. "Here you go miss, I'm sorry, I'm sorry," he said apologetically. I grabbed my purse from him and started going through it to make sure he did not take my money. By that time he had walked away, I didn't see my $40.00. So I called Sonny and Regaston from the back and told them the man had my money. We called the police and Regaston and I started down the street to look for him. Since we didn't see him on the block, we turned around and went back to the office.

In about ten minutes, a New York police patrol car pulled up and the officer said that his partner had stopped a man that fit the robber's description on the next block over. They wanted me to come and identify him. We jumped in the back seat and the officer sped-off. The speed, coupled with the dis-repair of the city's streets, had us bouncing around in the back seats.

"Is this the guy?" the officer asked as he stopped the police car with a shrieking halt.

"Yes, that's him." I got out of the car and kindly asked the man to give me my money back. The man assured me that he didn't take the money. The police then asked me what did I want to do. Since it was just $40.00 and the man had given my purse back, I told the officers to just let him go. Once I got back to the office and pulled everything out of my purse to see if the robber had taken anything else, I found my $40.00 at the bottom of the purse. I told everyone that I had found the money and that nothing else was missing from my purse. We went back to work.

The middle of August came and it was time for me to head back to Virginia. I had enjoyed a wonderful summer in New York with my family, my job, the ritzy parties with Jane Butel and the wonderful family stories from my cousin Sonny and Aunt Ethel. I had a new mindset about people. I had met people with brown skinned tones who spoke French. I had met people with olive skinned tones who spoke Spanish. I realized that things in New York were not just black and white like they were in the South. At one of Jane Butel's parties, I met an Asian man who had a Black wife and I met a West Indian man who had a white wife. Life was different and I was glad to have experienced diversity. I didn't leave the City of New York without a signature purse, a small burlap shoulder purse with "I Love New York" written on it. I just knew I was tough with my new purse and the fact I had made it through the entire summer in "The Big Apple."

Now, it was my sophomore year of college and this academic year would include more studies and my anticipation to pledge Alpha Kappa Alpha (AKA) Sorority, Incorporated. I had done all of the preliminaries—attended the RUSH, submitted my essay and met with the other members of the sorority, who would eventually become my "Big Sisters." I had the qualifications to be a member of the elite AKA sorority of the Theta Rho Chapter. What inspired me to look for the sorority once I got to college was the Lambda Omega Chapter in my hometown. During my senior year of high school, Lambda Omega Chapter of AKA along with Jessie M. Rattley, the first black female mayor of Newport News, had a special meeting at the Peninsula Business College, which she owned.

The meeting was to orientate attendees to college life. They chose the top five African-American female seniors from the following high schools: Menchville High, Warwick High, Denbigh High, and my alma mater Ferguson High. We met there on a Saturday at 9 o'clock in the morning. There were members of AKA sorority from Hampton Institute (known as Hampton University a/k/a "HU") and Christopher Newport College (known as Christopher Newport University a/k/a "CNU") who led discussions on college life and what we could expect. They were beautiful women in all shades of the African-American spectrum. Before we left the meeting, we each were given a special white seashell stuffed with a pink flower with green leaves. "I want each of you, when you get to your respective colleges and universities, to look on your campuses for the ladies of Alpha Kappa Alpha Sorority, Incorporated." the lead speaker stated as she bid us farewell and wished us much success as we left to continue our lives.

When Mom and I went to my freshman orientation, I did find the ladies in the "pink and green." Scholarship, leadership, character and sisterhood were what this national organization stood for and I wanted to be a part of it. I had definitely proven myself on the scholarship part. I was overwhelmed with joy from being the very first recipient of the Newport News Redevelopment and Housing Authority Scholarship in 1980 when the board decided to administer the award. The same year I went to college was the first year of the award. Because of my intelligence and community service, I was granted the award and received a $1,000 scholarship! Ms. Sandra Harris, the tenant relations advisor, worked with me through the application and interview process. To this day, this is one of my most decorated honors because it denoted just how I felt inside. Just because my family's income was low, did not mean my intelligence level was low.

"Well my interview is tomorrow," I told my friend Vickie who was from Ridgeway, Virginia. "I just hope they will accept me." I said.

"Me too, Tina," Vicki said. "Just try not to be nervous," she added. Vickie loved to tell people she was from Ridgeway because she knew nobody knew where the hell it was in Virginia. When you listened to her explain to others where it was located, she was proud to know her family members were the only ones who knew the whereabouts of Ridgeway, Virginia. "Tina you have what it takes—good grades, leadership and character. They need someone like you."

"I hope you are right, Vickie. We'll see." We stopped talking and finished our studies.

I made it through the interview and found out weeks later I was accepted. I had made the "Spring 1982 Ivy" line. It was time for an experience I would treasure for the rest of my life. We had to meet at "Big Sister" Trina's house one evening with black dresses, black pantyhose and black pumps, along with the traditional trench coats. At the meeting we were given our ivy pots and our line included nineteen smart ladies: Chantay Jones, Cynthia Cherry, Jackie Ingram, Ruth Hall, Bonita Carr, Denise Whitaker, Beverly Dameron, Annette Smith, Teunsha Williams, Eugenia Tolliver, Rita Taylor, Doris Bellamy, Marion Taylor, Nina Boone, Annette Jones, Cheryl Jones, Denean Ashe, Florence Canada, and me. We all became "A Scent of Arrogance." Our everyday togetherness lasted for a period of six weeks.

I had previously met a soror, Angela Bowser, whom I had kept in contact with over some years. She was the one I selected to pin me for my special night. I called my momma to let her know about the exciting night when I crossed over the golden sands of Alpha Kappa Alpha Sorority, Incorporated. She was excited about my accomplishment.

I kept my grades up in college and studied hard to make all A's and B's. I can remember dropping the History of the Civil War class. Unfortunately, I was lost in the class because the instructor was trying to glorify the Civil War. During my four years in college, that particular class was the only one from which I withdrew. My favorite class was the Economics and Poverty class. It was interesting finding out about social and class structure and how the world worked as it related to the "haves" and the "have nots." One day in class our instructor gave us an assignment.

"Sometimes you have to put yourself in other peoples' situation," said Professor Parker. "What I want everyone to do is to either live on a food stamp budget for a month, or go to one of the local soup lines and see how it feels to need a meal, then write about your experiences," he said.

One student who was in the auditorium style classroom, which seated approximately 75 people raised, his hand. "Do you have a list of the local soup lines?" the student asked. Since VCU was such a large university with over 30,000 students, most of us didn't know each other.

Mr. Parker replied, "Yes, I do. If you are interested and decide to use the soup line assignment, see me immediately after class and I will give you the information."

When Mr. Parker gave that assignment, the bubble over my head was reading . . . *I have been living on a food stamp budget for at least the last ten years of my life. That is nothing new for me.* I completed the assignment based on my real life experiences.

One of my most interesting professors was a nice-looking man named Dr. Norrece Jones, who came to VCU my junior year. My minor was African-American Studies and Dr. Jones was hired to teach within that department. All of the black students, who were activists, thought that he was hired because we had organized a rally at VCU to demand that administrators increase the black faculty at the university.

I took the History of West Africa class that he taught. He told us he was educated at Hampton University and Northwestern University. I couldn't understand it then, but he stressed to us the importance of networking. He gave all of the students his business card and told us to call him sometimes, if we had anything we needed to discuss. I was always thinking, "What in the world would we need to call him about?" That semester he had a gathering for the class which gave us all a chance to have small talk. Before I graduated, Dr. Jones secured an application for me to apply for a fellowship to work in the Governor's office. He was connecting me to an opportunity to which I never did apply because after graduation I was so ready to go home and be with my family. As I became older, my memory reflected back to those conversations he had with the class about meeting people. He was teaching us the importance of networking because he knew that we were going to need it to be successful.

Another one of my favorite professors was a lady by the name of Joyce Wise. She was one of the communications professors. She was very honest in her dealings with the students. I remember the first days of sitting in the class of Mass Communications 101. The second day of class, I was taking my notes, when I looked up and saw Ms. Wise pulling out a cigarette. She took a match and lit the cigarette. I looked around the classroom to see if anyone else thought it was strange that she was lighting that cigarette. I knew then I was not in high school anymore. Since nobody reacted in a negative way, I calmed down and pretended that this was normal behavior. I had no clue professors could smoke in class and I had never heard anyone mention that professors smoked in class. Right then and there, I knew that I was in college and in the big City of Richmond.

On that particular day we were discussing the type of voice broadcast journalist should have when they are on the air. "When you are a broadcast journalist, the public should not be able to tell where you are from and whether you are Black, White, Asian or Hispanic," Ms. Wise said. "It is important that you enunciate your words and do what we call objective reporting," she added.

I then raised my hand. "Ms. Wise, I want to "ax" you a question about . . ."

She abruptly stopped me. "Tina, what is this word?" she asked as she wrote on the chalkboard, A-S-K.

I said, "ax" because that is how I pronounced ask.

"No, it's A-S-K and start saying it," she demanded.

I was feeling kinda crazy, but I knew she wanted me to be the best in my field. After that experience, I did what she advised and purchased a tape recorder to hear myself speak. It worked because I could hear the imperfections in my use of the English language and I practiced hard to correct them.

I wanted to be the best news broadcaster. Ms. Wise seemed to like the fact that I tried to improve myself. The summer of my senior year in college, she referred me to an internship position that was with Channel 6 News in Richmond. It was at the upper end of West Broad Street and I learned how to catch the bus there. I enjoyed writing copy for the *Noon News* show and I did a voice-over for the morning weather. One of the reporters there helped me learn to talk for the weather voice-over because I sounded awful when I first began. I worked closely with the noon anchorman, Dennis Edwards. There was a tough female reporter at the station whose name was Maguarite Bardone. I admired her because even though it was a male dominated profession, she didn't take any junk from those men.

I finally purchased a car in my junior year of college. With the money from my internship I was able to buy a shiny, silver Pontiac Sunbird! I was glad to get my car before I graduated from college.

My four years of college went by fast and I found myself right on track to graduate. In 1984, I graduated with a Bachelor of Science in Communications. During my four years matriculation at VCU, I began to realize I was interested in three things: news reporting, local politics, and giving people information to improve their lives. My peers called me the humanitarian reporter because I was always reporting on people who needed a chance or were not being treated fairly. Although I always planned on building a successful career and traveling, I felt an obligation to my childhood home and community. Every break, during the summer, and holidays, I came home to spend time with my family. I finally decided that once I had completed my education, I would return to Newport News and do everything I could to improve the lives of people within my community.

CHAPTER FIVE

MY FAMILY

My family: Teunsha (5 years old) and
Terrance (3 years old) pictured w/Tina Vick

I was extremely disappointed in myself when I got pregnant.
I wanted to have that piece right in my life . . . not to have a baby
until I was married. I really didn't want that for my children. There
were numerous people who teased me and talked about me for
getting pregnant.

I was a substitute teacher at my old high school at this point, and I was working at Sears, Roebuck & Company (commonly known as Sears) part time nights and on Saturdays. Mrs. Moore was working with me at Sears one particular Saturday morning. She was an older lady who looked like a Native American with an olive complexion and mixed gray, wavy hair. We were folding the jeans in the Men's Department.

"My stomach is feeling nauseated and I had to throw up this morning before I left home," I told her.

"You not pregnant are you?" she asked.

"I don't think so," I answered as I wondered why that would be Mrs. Moore's first thought? "Why would you ask me that, Mrs. Moore?"

"Because it sounds like you are going through morning sickness," she said.

"I don't think I am." I had to work the entire Saturday, but I was not even thinking about being pregnant because it was the furthest thing on my mind.

Well, Mrs. Moore was right. I was pregnant. I went to the East End Clinic and the doctor confirmed I was approximately eight weeks pregnant. I hadn't even noticed I had skipped a period for the month of December of 1984. I didn't know what to do about the pregnancy. I was scared. I had finished college, but I did not have the good job that I thought I was going to get after obtaining my bachelor's degree. I was working as a substitute teacher and getting regular calls from my old high school. In order to supplement my income, I worked part-time at Sears in the Newmarket North Mall.

I didn't have the ideal situation. I always wanted to be married before I had children. I just wanted to do things the right way. After much discussion and turmoil, I decided to keep my baby and deal with having my child out of wedlock. Unfortunately, I didn't want to tell my momma because I knew she expected more out of me. I couldn't keep the secret any longer, after February, because my teeny-tiny waist started to expand and my breasts begin to explode.

My chest looked like the country singer, Dollie Pardon's breasts. When anyone looked at me, they knew something was different.

I had told my boyfriend, Wayne the same day I came home from my doctor's appointment. He was angry. Wayne and I had met in my junior year of college, but it was nothing serious until I had graduated from college and came back home. His real name was Calvin Wayne Knight. He was one of the best looking men in Newport News. We spent many days and nights together and we shared some great times. We had many discussions regarding whether or not I should go through with the pregnancy. After all, I was an adult who had received a college degree.

One day after Momma had finished watching her soap operas, or "stories" as she called them, I decided to tell her.

"Momma are you busy, I need to tell you something."

"I'm just sitting here waiting for the news to come on," she said.

"I'm having a baby," I stated.

"I thought you were looking strange and I started to ask you about that," she said. "Are you and Wayne gonna get married?"

"No, we are not getting married right now Momma," I said.

"Well, ya'll need to get married because you know if you don't they gone make you stop working at the school!" she said. I started crying because I could tell Momma was mad. I was hurt that I had disappointed her.

The next day I went to work at the school and I went in the office to talk to Mrs. Ford. "Good morning, Mrs. Ford, how are you doing?"

"Good Morning Tina, I'm doing fine. Are you here for your class assignment?"

"I already have it Mrs. Ford, but I need to talk to you before class starts."

"Sure, come on in my office and we can talk," she said smiling.

Mrs. Nancy Ford was the secretary at Homer L. Ferguson High School for years. She was a small framed lovely brunette, with the cutest hairstyle that was cut in a bob. She was friendly to everyone and she always had a smile on her face. She sat down behind her cherry wood desk and folded her hands and looked at me with a smile.

"What can I help you with?" she asked.

"Well, I am pregnant and I am not going to be getting married."

"Will I have to stop working here as a substitute teacher?" I asked nervously.

She looked at me almost in shock. "No! You don't have to stop working here. You do a great job for us and as long as you can work, we will keep calling you," she said.

"Thank you, Mrs. Ford. I wanted to be upfront and honest about my situation," I said.

"I appreciate it Tina, but just continue teaching until it is time to have your baby."

"Well, let me get to class, before the students get here," I told her.

"Okay, now you have a great day." Mrs. Ford told me as I left her office.

I was so relieved to know I wouldn't lose my job. I just couldn't wait to go home and tell my momma.

I was still feeling bad about being pregnant and not getting married. It was difficult for me mentally. It was strange to see that when I had been doing good things people were happy for me and saying good things. Then when I made this mistake, I felt like the whole neighborhood was against me. I was very mad at myself.

One day as I was sitting at home, I kept seeing this commercial stating, "if you need prayer or counseling, call *The 700 Club*." *The 700 Club* is a religious organization headed by Marion Gordon "Pat" Robertson. They had a "1-800" toll free number which I wrote down and called to speak with a counselor.

"Hello, you've reached *The 700 Club*," she said.

I was very nervous, but I talked anyway. "Hi, I . . . I just called for prayer because I am having a baby and I am not married. I feel really bad," I told the counselor who was a woman.

"God bless you and thank you for calling," the counselor said.

"I just don't know what to do," I informed her.

"Well, I know you are nervous and undecided. God hates the sin, but he loves you and your baby very, very much," she said.

To this very day, I can remember those words because they made me feel freed from my burden. I don't remember anything about what she said after that; I just remember feeling like a weight had been lifted off of me. I knew I could make it with my baby. I began crying, but I kept listening to the counselor.

"You stay strong and be a good mother to your child," she said.

"Thank you for your prayers and I feel much better," I said.

God blessed me to carry my pregnancy to full term. I had the most beautiful baby girl in the world, Teunsha Lynette Vick. She was 8 pounds and 4 ounces with a pecan complexion and curly black hair. My daughter was born at Riverside General Hospital (known today as Riverside Regional Medical Center). All of the nurses there were saying how beautiful she was. After her birth, the nurses who cleaned her up said it looked like she had gotten her hair done prior to being delivered. We looked at each other eye-to-eye making our mother-daughter connection. The doctor gave me a Cesarean section (C-section) because I was in labor for over sixteen hours and I had only dilated one and a half centimeters.

My daughter's father, Wayne, came to the hospital to tell me that his mother had died on the same day that Teunsha was born. He was very sad. I can remember the look upon his face signaling that he didn't know which way to go or even which way to turn. For us, that particular day was a joyful one because our beautiful daughter had come into the world, but yet a sorrowful one because Wayne's mother had left the world. With great empathy, I told him, "I'm so sorry to hear that."

I had always told my sorority sister, Teunsha (whom we affectionately called "Shay") that if I ever had a daughter—she would be named, "Teunsha." When I said that, I truly don't think she paid me any attention because we were both in college and neither of us were even thinking about having any children at that time. Well, I kept my promise.

After Teunsha was born, we had the best life. I loved being with her. I only wanted to go to one job, so I could be at home with my baby in the evenings. Wayne and I did what we could to make our baby's life a good one. She was steadily growing up, learning how to talk quickly and reaching all of her developmental milestones on time.

Since my niece Niki was accustomed to being with me, she had to adjust to Teunsha. When Teunsha was about six months, she was with Niki and began crying badly as if she were in severe pain. I had gone in the kitchen to grab Teunsha's bottle.

"Niki, what happened to Teunsha?" I asked.
Niki looked around nervously and said, "I pinched her."
"Why did you do that?"
She kindly replied, "Cuz, I was jealous."
I told her she didn't have to be jealous because I would always make time for her and love her just as much.

As Teunsha got older, we called her "Tee." She loved to sing and by the age of three, she knew all of Anita Baker's songs. Her daddy loved to hear her sing the songs. She would sing like a little superstar. As her parents, we thought that she was the most beautiful child in the world. As her mother, she was the love of my life. I took her everywhere with me and I was a proud mother of this beautiful daughter whom I loved with all of my heart.

Single parenting didn't seem that difficult for me because I had seen so many women in my neighborhood do it and handle it very well. It goes back to what I call my "Tunnel Vision Theory." The theory is that the top five or ten things in your life that you see every day become the main factors with the most influence. As a result, those factors become your world and/or your reality. Living in public housing and single parenting is a part of the world that becomes your reality. There were many women mastering it and even though you knew the biblical way was to be married, something in your mind told you, "It's okay to have a baby and make it on your own." I'm not advocating that single-parenting is the right thing to do, but that is the mentality of most of the people who grew up like I did.

Now that I had a daughter, I wanted to find a decent job where I made enough money not to need a second job. I had finished college and I desired a job making at least a $30,000 salary to have a good life for me and my daughter. During the eighties, if you found work paying that kind of salary, you landed a good job. I knew I was smart and should be earning at least that much money.

When I graduated from college, I had applied everywhere within the City of Newport News. I thought that my college education would have landed me a good paying job. Unfortunately, nothing happened for me. When I would talk to some of my friends who were white, they were landing jobs. Their parents were connected so they only had to make a phone call to their friends and, like magic, their children would get hired. I couldn't believe this was happening. I began to think harder about why my former professor, Dr. Norrece Jones, taught us how to network at Virginia Commonwealth University (VCU). Dr. Jones had already learned what it took and was trying to teach us the significance of networking. I thought the degree was an instant ticket to a better life. I didn't know anything about the politics of life and being in a special network to get a job.

One day my friend Billie Stephens and I were so fed up about not finding a job that we went to every business from the base of Newport News, located at 6th Street and Jefferson Avenue to the Denny's Restaurant a little past West Mercury Boulevard on Jefferson Avenue. He had just graduated from the University of Virginia (UVA). We said we were not going to stop until somebody hired us on that particular day. I didn't want to think this, but it seemed like once employers saw what area I lived in, they just didn't want to hire me. Our search ended at the Denny's because the manager hired Billy and me on the spot.

I was really glad to get that full-time waitress position. Even though I knew I was over qualified, I needed a job to make more money to help me to live. With this job, I could be at home in the evenings with my daughter. I loved working at Denny's and I worked hard there as if I was the CEO of my own company. I began getting customers who only wanted to have me as their waitress. I had one couple who worked in the shipyard that would call me to prepare a table for them because they only had forty-five minutes and they knew I would give them excellent customer service.

I had many fond memories working a job I knew I was over qualified to do. I had work experience from working summer jobs at the VCU library and at the campus radio station. Now with a college degree, I was a waitress. Some days it would get to me emotionally. I would think about how I had done all of that studying and this is where it landed me.

One day, I had the honor and privilege of serving Bishop Samuel L. Green and his crew from St. John's Church of God in Christ which was located downtown in Newport News. He came with approximately seven people in his holy entourage.

"We got to get the Bishop his breakfast!" the gentleman told me as I seated all of them. "He needs to get his breakfast," he said.
"I can help you," I replied.

Most of the waitresses didn't want to wait on what we called the "church people." On Sundays, they would come and have dinner and sit in our stations for hours. They would eat and keep us running for more tea and soda. They would drink gallons of tea because the refills on the tea and even sodas were absolutely free. Most of the time there were at least six people in the party. After sitting for at least three hours, they would walk out and leave the waitress just a single one dollar bill. I really hoped that wouldn't be the case this particular morning.

"Let me take your order," I said politely. Each of the people in the party told me what they wanted to order and I took it to the cook. "Can you put a rush on this order Betty?" I asked.

"I'll make it as fast as I can," she said.

I got the Bishop and his entourage their drinks. The breakfast didn't take long so I was able to serve them quickly. I waited on them hand and foot giving them great service with my upbeat personality. I had already been thinking earlier that day about making enough money to pay my rent. I kept checking on the Bishop and all of his guests. They must have been extremely satisfied with my service because when I was about to return to the table, one of his people met me at the service table. He had filled the condiment bowl where we keep the sugar and the artificial sweeteners, with money.

"On behalf of Bishop Green, we want to thank you for your service and we appreciate you getting the Bishop his breakfast," he said.

"Oh, thank you so much, but I was just doing my job," I insisted.

"You did a great job and we thank you," he replied.

"Ya'll have a good day, and thank you for dining at Denny's," I said as they walked out of the restaurant.

I went to the back to count my money and they had left me over sixty dollars in tips for those seven people. I was happy as hell!!! I started telling everybody about my fortune. As waitresses, we used to keep our tips in our skirt pockets, but it was so many dollars that it made my brown Denny's skirt lean to one side. I was ready to get off and pack up for the day, but I had to finish my shift.

There was one other day which was memorable. At the end of my shift, I was wiping off all of the tables in my section and filling up all of the condiments. There was a man sitting in one of my booths relaxing after finishing his meal. We were just talking about life. I told him I had been to college and how hard it was finding a job.

I didn't get his name, but he said, "You know I admire you because so many people would not work a job like this if they had a degree. They would rather stay at home until they found a job that they qualified for."

"Well, I thank you. But, all money spends," I replied.

"I know that's right and you keep up the good work," he said as he drank his last cup of coffee.

I think God had sent him in Denny's that day as encouragement for me, because I just couldn't believe I had been working there for over a year since I couldn't find another job in my field. We were like a family at the restaurant. Although we had some good times, I needed to make money. I always kept thinking that I should have stayed in Richmond, Virginia.

Wayne and I stayed together. After 18 months, I was pregnant with another baby, my adorable son, Terrance Leonard Vick. I was still working at Denny's. They had given me a brown maternity dress when I was pregnant with my son whom I fondly nicknamed "Felix." I worked the 7:00 a.m. to 3:00 p.m. shift every morning. As soon as I got there, I would pour an eight ounce glass of milk and drink the whole thing. The milk was good and cold. As soon as I would get the milk down, Felix would start kicking in my stomach real hard. When I was taking the customers food orders, I felt like they could see my dress moving from him kicking inside. Felix was letting me know that he was alive and strong and couldn't wait to come out of my womb and join the Vick Family.

My son, Terrance was born on March 18, 1987. He was a little handsome baby that weighed seven pounds and nine ounces.

When I had him by another C-Section that day, I was excited to see him, because the doctor had told me I was having a boy. When I had Teunsha, I was surprised when she was born because I had informed the doctor that I did not want to know if I was pregnant with a boy or a girl. Felix was the cutest thing with his fuzzy, black hair and light skin tone like his father. Immediately after my son was born, he looked into my eyes as if he knew who I was. I chose to breast feed him because I knew he would be my last baby and if I didn't breastfeed with him, I would not have a chance. The breastfeeding nurse from Riverside General Hospital, Ms. Linda Hahn, made regular appointments with me to ensure that I was not having any problems.

By this time I had moved from Heritage Trace apartments located in Newport News in an area called "Denbigh" back down to Ridley Circle into a public housing apartment. The apartment was approximately three doors down from the apartment that I grew up in located on 12th Street. One day my momma sat down with me to tell me that she was not going to keep both of my children so I could go back to work. Since my children were born so close in age, I would have to stay at home with them. My heart sank to hear this news. I loved working and I just wasn't ready to stop. I really had enjoyed my maternity leave because it helped me get adjusted to parenting two children.

During my maternity leave, I kept searching for jobs that paid more. If I could make more money, I would be able to afford daycare for Felix and Tee. Fortunately, I had found a job as a counselor with pregnant teens that allowed me to work from home. The job was with the same agency that I had worked for as a youth. The Board of Directors had changed its name from the Office of Economic Opportunity to the Office of Human Affairs. Yes, thank God!!! I had found a professional job! No welfare for me! I raised my own babies and was a good mother to them. We spent a lot of time together and my children were the joy of my life. My daughter, Tee, was a bundle of joy who grew up loving to entertain people and my son, Felix, was a little man who knew, at an early age, he was around to love and protect his mom and sister.

Unfortunately, things didn't work out with Wayne and me. By the time we ended our relationship, I was an outreach counselor for the Peninsula Marine Institute (PMI). The program was a day treatment program for juvenile offenders from ages 14 to 18. I had worked there for approximately four years, when a promotion became available with an opportunity for me to go to New Orleans, Louisiana, South Carolina or Florida. I had prayed and asked God to send me to whichever place I would make the biggest impact and to allow everything to work out (i.e. salary, transportation). I transitioned from PMI to the New Orleans Marine Institute (NOMI). I uprooted my children at the ages of 5 and 7 and went further south, destined for a better life and new opportunities. We packed up and I drove to New Orleans in a U-Haul. I had no family there, but went for a better job opportunity. My babies made the adjustment and we started enjoying our lives in a new place.

Laura Axtell, the executive director of the program, hired me for the position in New Orleans. On the first day that my children and I arrived, Laura took us to the historic French Quarter. While there, we visited the French Market where she bought us our first pound of crawfish. We sat on the curb, in the market learning how to eat them and no one even noticed us. There were thousands of people walking around, enjoying shopping, and being filled with the excitement of the French Quarter. We even tasted the beignets (french-style doughnuts covered with powdered sugar) at Café Du Monde—they were so delicious. I had never eaten them before, but hundreds of people crowded that coffee shop located on Decatur Street. This café is best known for its beignets and coffee. Traditionally, their coffee is served black or Au Lait (mixture of half coffee and hot milk) with chicory. Chicory is the root of the endive plant. When roasted and grounded, it is added to the coffee to soften the bitter edge of dark roasted coffee. Café Du Monde's coffee served with Au Lait and chicory is called "Café Au Lait."

We left for New Orleans at the end of January, right at the Mardi Gras season. This place was definitely not like my home State of Virginia. If a street was closed for a parade, they would close the street and not have any detour signs to show the new route. I guess they thought everybody was from New Orleans, so they blocked the street traffic as if it was normal. I had to figure out how to get back to the Posada Del Rey apartments in Metairie where we lived. I lived in the City of Metairie and worked in the 9th Ward area of New Orleans.

My babies were growing up Cajun. When Felix went to school and brought home this little naked plastic doll baby, I had no clue what that meant. When I took him to school the next day, I asked the teacher.

She said, "Oh Ms. Vick, when anyone gets the baby in the King Cake, it is your responsibility to bring the King Cake the next day."

"Oh Mrs. Duncan, I am very sorry I am not from here, and had no idea of the Mardi Gras' tradition."

"Oh that's understandable," she replied.

"But I will bring the King Cake tomorrow," I informed her.

"Oh that's fine Ms. Vick," she said, "We will enjoy it whenever you bring it."

As I left the classroom, my thoughts were, "What in the hell is a King Cake?" When I got to my office, I asked my co-workers. The secretary started laughing. Being from New Orleans, it was very hard for her to even imagine anyone not knowing what a King Cake was.

"Oh, the King Cake is a special cake for Mardi Gras. It's like a big cinnamon roll with icing on the top. The icing is made in the Mardi Gras colors of yellow, purple and green," Wanda informed me.

"Well, I have to buy one for Felix's class," I said.

"You can buy one from the Schwegmann Bakery," Wanda replied and continued to laugh.

This was a strange culture not to mention I had moved to Metarie which was the home of David Duke, the head master of the Ku Klux Klan. It was going to take some getting used to this area of the nation. Once I had gotten my children into school, the administrators had given me the paperwork with the rules and regulations of the schools. I looked at all of the forms, including the school menu. As part of the menu, they were serving my babies red beans and rice. I could not believe they were giving the children beans. I was mad because when I was growing up in Virginia, if your family ate beans, it meant you had a lot of children and you were trying to stretch the meal, or you were poor and didn't have anything else to cook for a meal.

As a concerned parent, I called the New Orleans Public School System administrative office to ask why they were giving my babies beans!

"Good Morning, this is Tina Vick and I want to speak with whoever is in charge of the students' lunch menu," I said.

"Good Morning," the receptionist said, "I will make the connection."

I didn't catch the name as to who I was talking to, but I know I made it loud and clear that I was disappointed that they had red beans and rice on the school menu. I wanted to know what I could do about it. The secretary just held the phone. I wondered why she seemed reluctant to respond to my complaint. She didn't know why I was complaining because red beans and rice was a delicacy for the residents of New Orleans. After she explained it, I understood. Being from Virginia, I couldn't recall any school day where beans were on the menu. I actually couldn't believe I was in a place where beans were a delicacy.

When we were down in the French Quarter, we went to Emeril's Restaurant. I was appalled to see one of his top dishes was red beans and rice. White table cloths decorated this elegant restaurant owned by a top rated chef and beans were a specialty on his menu! What a difference in the regions of the United States. I knew I was in a different part of America.

Well, it didn't take us long to get use to our life in New Orleans, Louisiana. I met so many nice people. The NOMI crew became my extended family. I had moved there for a promotion as the family services coordinator. My primary responsibility was to recruit juveniles who had been adjudicated into our day treatment program and provide educational and behavioral services. Our program also combined the use of water related activities to lead the kids on the right path. The team of professionals at NOMI engaged the youth to help them understand crime was not the answer to a successful life. I did an outstanding job. My predecessor, with her master of social work degree, said she could not get many students to qualify for the program. I had a bachelor's degree, but I worked hard and met with the probation officers and interviewed the parents. Before my six months probationary period ended, I had a waiting list of youth to enroll in our program. She also said she had been holding parenting workshops, and the parents would not come out. When I scheduled my first parenting workshop, I contacted each parent directly and arranged transportation. As a result, my first parent meeting was standing room only. From the few things I had accomplished, I realized that it doesn't matter what degrees you have, if you care about people and are willing to work hard, you can make things happen. I really wanted to make a difference in the lives of people. At the meeting, I was the presenter and my children, Tee and Felix, sat on the front row. As I was speaking, whenever I looked at the both of them, they kept making funny faces to make me laugh.

I was able to get to New Orleans early enough to enroll my children in a great school and they got a good education. My babies grew up and did amazing things. Tee was involved in the cheerleading, which led her in the Mardi Gras parades with the F.W. Gregory Elementary School. Felix was an amazing school artist and the protector of the family. He was featured in *The Times-Picayune*, the city's newspaper, as a child artist when he attended Dr. Martin Luther King Elementary School.

I have always loved the big city. It was a little difficult not having my mother around, but I just wanted to make a better life for me and my children. I had an upscale apartment which included tennis courts, a swimming pool and a balcony. Unlike when I was in Virginia living on the Section 8 Rental Assistance Program, I had a nice place in Bellwood Apartments. Section 8 is a special public housing program, through the federal government, which allows low-income families, elderly, and disabled to rent affordable housing in the private housing sector. I called the office to let my representative know I was moving to Louisiana. Before I left, she informed me that the voucher was transferable from state to state. Since my salary had increased with my promotion and I trusted in God, I informed her that I was not transferring the voucher to Louisiana. I was confident that I could make it on my own. For me, this was the end of my life on government assistance. I was leaving the poverty life behind me.

The job was great. Thanks to my good friend Wanda Polk, I was able to navigate my way around the city. She helped me learn the streets of New Orleans and warned me about going through the downtown projects (located in the ninth ward) like the Desire and Florida and also the uptown projects like the Calliope (located in the second ward) and the Melpomene (located in the third ward). There were plenty of gold teeth and alcohol around in those areas. One thing I noticed was unlike the children in Virginia who had gotten into trouble and had the opportunity to enroll in the program; however, they usually had high academic testing scores. But not in New Orleans! I had never seen so many 16 to 18 year old boys testing on second and third grade academic and reading levels. With such low reading and math scores, it was evident of a systematic problem within the New Orleans public schools systems. Our instructors worked very hard with those students to improve their reading levels.

Wanda and I began going walking and shopping together. We attended her church, Greater Power Baptist Church. It was a small church in the seventh ward. The service was at 8 in the morning and I was not used to an early church service. Tee started singing in the children's choir. I enrolled Felix in the choir too, but instead of singing during the services, he would sleep; therefore, I had to go to his seat and wake him up. I dressed Felix in silk shirts and pleated pants and he used to look so handsome, but he would constantly fall asleep in the choir stand. He would sleep so hard that he would not even know when the choir would stand to sing. Everyone in the choir would be standing up and my son would be slumped over fast asleep. At the church Wanda's son, Matthew played the drums and did so exceptionally well. He was also an excellent student in school.

Matthew's nickname was "Bubba" and we cheered him on as he would beat those drums to some of the best gospel music in New Orleans. Wanda and her husband, Craig, had a daughter named Candice. Craig was a very kind man. They would invite my family over whenever he cooked fried chicken and made his special gumbo.

My children and I would take walks on the Riverwalk. It seemed that every Saturday New Orleans was having some kind of festival which we attended. My friend Andrea called me the festival queen. My children loved being outside and finding out new things about a new culture. I couldn't get over the horse and buggy rides which allowed visitors to see historic areas in the French Quarter. I loved the way the tour guides talked with that heavy New Orleans accent which made the stories even more interesting. New Orleans had such an entrepreneurial spirit because there were all types of ways to do business there. I will never forget one man in the French Quarter who would sell disposable cameras and rain ponchos.

Tee and Felix were steadily growing and moving along in school. Even though we lived in Metairie, which was a suburb of New Orleans, we spent much time in the city. I would go to the city to find a beautician to style me and my daughter's hair and a barber to cut my son's hair. Felix was very particular about the way he looked. He was handsome and loved to look good. In the morning when I got him dressed for school, I would sing the song "He's a Knock Out" to him. I would clap my hands and sing, "He wears the finest designer clothes around, he's the baddest dresser in this town, he's so tall lean and slim, no other kids can come close to him! He's a knock out, he's so fine, and he's mine all mine." He would look at me like I was crazy as I sang to him. Felix was my suave and debonair son. As he got older, he became more and more handsome and grew into my little man.

Felix did not like school because he wanted to be at home with me and Teunsha. I had to tell him repeatedly that I was going to work and Tee was going to school. He did not want to study and preferred playing outside instead. However, he was a magnet for friends. He loved playing with his friends: Peanut, Tippy and Chris. He had the best personality. Unfortunately, it seemed like all of his friends had irresponsible mothers who were doing their own thing as their children were getting older. I ended up as the driver for all of his friends. I would take them to the movies, CiCi's Pizza Parlor and to the French Quarter. They enjoyed themselves.

Felix also loved animals—dogs, turtles, lizards and iguanas. I had to get used to animals because of him. When we had left New Orleans briefly to go to Norfolk, Virginia, he wanted a dog. We were living in an apartment and a dog would not have enough space to move around. I told Felix we could not afford a dog right at that time and he broke down crying. He could not accept that we couldn't have a dog in our tiny two bedroom apartment.

The apartment was in Chesapeake, Virginia and not far from my job in Norfolk. We didn't live in Chesapeake for a long time because, mentally, I was not ready to be back in Virginia. My children were enrolled in the Chesapeake Public Schools System and afterschool program. One evening, as we were sitting around the dinner table, Teunsha said she didn't want to go back to the afterschool program because the children did not want to play with them because they were black. Felix said the same thing and told me that they were in the corner playing by themselves. The afterschool program was at a predominantly white church, but my mind did not believe a church program would be practicing rascism. The worst thing was that she told me this after the daycare was closed for the day. I was so angry that I could barely sleep that night because I could not wait to get to the church the next day.

It was 1995 and I could not believe the experiences I was having living in Chesapeake, Virginia. Because at the same time that the afterschool situation was going on, I had another racial situation to occur. One day as I was checking the messages on my answering service, there was a message from some man who did not realize he had not hung up his phone. My answering machine recorded him saying, "Honey, this ain't Billy's house, this some nigger's house." Apparently, they had called me back from a message that I had left about the program. I could not believe what I was hearing. Here it was at least thirty years after the Civil Rights Act of 1964 and someone was leaving a message like this on my answering machine. I was appalled.

As soon as the church afterschool program opened that very next day, I called to tell them what my children had informed me. The administrator assured me that was not the case. I was upset and could not believe we were going through this. Maybe because I was a child of the period of integration and as a result, I had my views on equality for all. Therefore, I just could not grasp this racism. I believed my children and I was not going to take a chance on them being treated unfairly. I told them I wanted my registration fees back, as well as what I had paid for the first two weeks. I was glad my children were able to verbalize what they experienced. I took them immediately out of that church day care. It is just something about being a parent. When people mess with me that is different because I can hold my own, but when someone picks with my children, it is all out war! I was very upset and wanted justice to be served. I couldn't believe I would have to deal with this in the church program designed for children. I vowed I would only be in Virginia for a while, to get the Norfolk Marine Institute up and running, and then I would be on my way back to the "Big Easy."

I reconnected with my good friend from college, Tima Smith. Tima remained in Richmond, Virginia after college and got a good job as a nurse. Tima's mom and dad lived in Portsmouth, Virginia. All of the cities were intertwined. Tima's mom, Ethel, agreed to watch my children afterschool. I just loved the Smith Family and we began spending more time with them. Mr. Smith was like a father to me. When I would come home from school for the weekends, after I had gotten my Pontiac Sunbird, Mr. Smith would take my car keys and check the vehicle's tires, windshield wipers and oil. Kim, Nicole, Tippy and I would talk for hours. Tima's brother Scott, who I use to affectionately call "Scott O'Lad" was the best. My children loved being with the Smiths and my mind was at ease. I was glad to reconnect with the entire Smith Family.

After the Norfolk Marine Institute was up and running, I had plans for me and my children to head back to New Orleans, Louisiana. Before leaving, my family had received word from my paternal grandmother that our dad was very ill. While I was still in Virginia, my father passed away. Unfortunately, we had not seen him much since the separation and divorce from our mom. My dad had relocated to the State of Texas and begun a whole new life for himself. When my mom told me that he had died, I had no sad reaction. Even though I know we had his blood in our veins, I just didn't feel sorrowful. All I kept thinking about was how men who had children needed to think about life at the end of the tunnel. If you aren't a Daddy to your children and not spending time with them, you can't think that your children are going to be depressed when you die. I hated that I could not grieve, but I just couldn't help it. For years, he had not been a part of our family's lives. I wasn't going to fake and act like things were alright, when they weren't.

Imbedded in my mind, which I will never forget, are the words that my dad said to my mom that I overheard. He said he couldn't have anything because of us. I couldn't believe that he said those things and we were his blood. I did attend his funeral along with my sisters, my mom and my brother Casey. Joe Jr. was in jail, as he usually was, so he didn't go. I sat there at the funeral, but since it had been so many years without any interaction, it felt like I was attending a stranger's funeral because it was the right thing to do. My dad did say that he couldn't have anything because of us; yet he had been without us for all of those years and did not even have "two brown pennies to rub together." My grandma asked us if we wanted to have any of his clothes and neckties. I certainly did not. He should have left us an inheritance and not any damn old clothes.

CHAPTER SIX

THE BIG DECISION

While I was making a life for myself and children in New Orleans, my nephew Michael was developing into a great athlete. By his senior year in high school, he was being recruited by colleges and universities. Everyone in the family had opinions about what college he should choose. We were advised by Coach Reamon, Michael's high school coach, not to say too much about our opinions on which college he should choose because it needed to be his decision. As a result I kept my mouth shut about the school, but I made sure I told him to go somewhere with great academics, but also a place he would be comfortable socially. Really, I thought he should have chosen Syracuse University, because it was a popular university. The school also had much visibility and the football coaches were courting Michael to attend. When he chose Virginia Polytechnic Institute and State University, popularly known as Virginia Tech (VA Tech), I was surprised. My memory of Virginia Tech was in the late seventies, when Blacks from my hometown of Newport News were careful about going there because it was too far from the Peninsula area, there were not many black students attending the school and based on the reports from my friends, you could not even get any black radio stations out there. But I soon found out the VA Tech team was dedicated to its motto, Ut Prosim (That I May Serve).

The school was located in Blacksburg, Virginia and consisted of eight colleges and graduate schools. It boasted having 65 bachelor's degree programs and 150 master's and doctoral degree programs. Unlike in the seventies and eighties, when Michael attended the university had 30,000 plus full-time students and a dedicated alumni program. Their main campus included more than 125 buildings, 2,600 acres and an airport. Included on the campus was a corporate research center. It had been ranked 47th among research universities in the United States. The staff was about teamwork and they were wonderful and very attentive to Michael. According to Michael's mother, my sister Brenda, his leaving was one of the saddest times of their lives. Even though the family was happy about Michael's opportunity, they did not want him to be five hours away from home.

During this time, Coach Reamon was a tremendous counselor to Michael. According to Michael, he shared his experiences about the National Football League (NFL) and college football so Michael could understand about his new life. Michael entered VA Tech as a redshirt freshman, which meant that he would sit on the bench for the first year to study the game of football and the second year, he would be able to play. He would not be involved in any other sport. His focus would be concentrating on his studies and football.

I have to confess that even though he was a great athlete, it never crossed my mind that Michael would become a professional football player. I remember the days when Coach Bernard Johnson at the Boys and Girls Club, coached all of the young boys, including Michael and his brother, Marcus. They were affectionately known as the "Vick Boys." Coach Johnson was a very handsome brown skinned man who always kept himself in good shape. As he yelled assignments out on the practice field, the sun would glisten on his wavy, black hair. He was always very serious about working with the Vick boys. I remember the times that he would pay the registration fees for them when my sister did not have the money. He was dedicated to making a winning team.

On some Saturday mornings, he would come and pick up Michael and Marcus in this old, noisy retired school bus that had been donated to the Boys and Girls Club. The bus definitely served its purpose, it was full of young black males. The sounds of their constant chatter would permeate through the windows. "Come on Mike and Marcus!!! Let's go!" Coach Johnson would yell. My nephews would run out of the house with all of their equipment and uniforms, ready to go. They just loved football. I honestly believe Michael got the strength of throwing the football from all of the rocks he threw over the roof of the Ridley Circle Apartments. Michael, who I affectionately called "Oogie," used to loved to stand in the middle of the oval circle located on 12th Street and find rocks to throw to the other side of the entire row of apartments.

Oogie did his thing at VA Tech once his redshirt agreement had come to an end. His first year on the field, he led the VA Tech Hokies to victory after victory against Boston College, West Virginia, and University of Virginia (UVA). He and the Hokie team, along with Andre Davis, Corey Moore and Shayne Graham, outperformed any team in VA Tech history! At the game against Rutgers University, my nephew soared into the end zone, did a somersault and landed on his feet for a touchdown. The crowd went wild! Even the announcers were saying, "This guy is like Superman!" Little did we know that he was changing the course of VA Tech football forever.

When my family came from New Orleans to go to our first college game, we were excited. VA Tech was playing against Boston College. There was orange and burgundy everywhere. Coach Beamer greeted my sister and I along with his athletic director, Sharon Shavensky.

"Hello Brenda!" he said joyously and gave her a big hug. Coach Beamer just loved Brenda and the Tech family took good care of her when she went out to the games.

"Coach Beamer, this is my sister, Tina," Brenda said. "She is here visiting from New Orleans."

"Oh, nice to meet you!" he said and gave me a hug too. "I certainly can see the resemblance," he said laughing.

"We're only a year apart!" I told him as I laughed.

I had been saying that all of our lives because people always said Brenda and I looked just alike. Many times people thought we were twins. After we sat around on the beautiful tan leather sofas and chatted for awhile, they transported us into the stadium on golf carts. We stopped at the concession area and Sharon took us to our seats.

When the family went to the games, the news reporters from the Blacksburg stations and ESPN loved to interview my sister about her son, Michael. Brenda hated being interviewed and on television.

"Brenda, why won't you talk to the television reporters about the games and Oogie?" I asked.

"I don't feel like talking to those people; I just wanna watch the game," she said.

"You know you need to say something to the press about Oogie! It's not like they can ask you any trick questions because you have known him all of his life," I said laughing.

Brenda laughed and said," Well, I don't care. I don't like talking on the camera." Despite her unwillingness to talk to them, they still put Brenda's face on the television screen when they talked about Michael. I found it to be funny because no matter how much she tried, she still could not escape the reporters. They were interested in finding out about Michael's upbringing because they were amazed by his performance at the games. Even at that Boston game, Oogie and the Hokies made so many good plays that people could barely sit in their seats. As soon as one play started, the crowd thought Oogie had gotten tackled, but he finagled away from those players and was up and running again!! Tee and Felix and I were screaming and jumping up and down because we just couldn't believe it was Oogie!!

"Go Oogie!! You doing your thang, Ook!" I screamed!
Felix chimed in, "Mike Vick!!!! You doing it!!

At the end of the season this new quarterback, Michael Vick, had led the team to an 11-0 season. My nephew was amazing! It was on to the Sugar Bowl. The Virginia Tech Hokies coached by Frank Beamer were headed to New Orleans, Louisiana to compete with Bobby Bowden and the Florida State Seminoles for the Sugar Bowl championship!!!!

At that time, I was employed at Hilton New Orleans Riverside Hotel as a training assistant in the Human Resources Department.

We received word that the Hokie team would be staying at the Hilton for the Sugar Bowl.

"Hey Alvina! My nephew, Michael, and the VA Tech team will be staying here for the Sugar Bowl!!!!! Yeah!! I cannot wait until he gets here!" I said.
"I hope I get to meet him," Alvina said.
"Sure thing, Alvina. I'll make sure that you do," I promised.

Weeks went by as everyone made preparations for the classic Sugar Bowl. Banners were in the hotel lobby which read "Welcome Hokies to the Hilton."

The New Orleans Marine Institute (NOMI) which brought me to New Orleans, had shut down because of a lack of funds. It seems the program's management system supported the people who needed a crutch instead of the smart people who were capable. I tried to work my way up to an executive director but the job was given to people who were less capable. However, they always wanted me to help train the person for the position. The management knew of my interest and aspirations, but did not want to give me an opportunity. While I was working at NOMI, there were three opportunities where the executive director position became available and I was denied the opportunity each time.

Before the third exec was hired, I had one of the most degrading encounters with one of the regional directors. It was a warm day with a slight overcast. I was up early because I wanted to put my name in the hat for the executive director position. Upon arrival to the institute, Mr. Russell called me into the classroom in the middle of the hallway.

"Tina, I know you are interested in the job, but you're not going to get that job. You're not going to get that job unless God himself comes down. You're just not going to get it," he stated firmly. Then he left the room. I was shocked and speechless, because I thought we could at least have some type of dialogue. Well, about 30 days later, God himself did come down and the State of Louisiana didn't renew the funding. The program was forced to close within the next 30 days. I wanted an opportunity to tell Mr. Russell, "I guess you see God came down because you didn't give me an opportunity at the executive director position." I thought.

Finally, after the third time, I filed a grievance within the company. Several of the Associated Marine Institute (AMI) administrators came to New Orleans to conduct an investigation. They offered me a chance to enroll in a leadership program. I declined the offer.

Since we had to close NOMI, I received three months of severance pay. It was perfect timing because it was during the summer so I didn't have to work. I had a great summer with my children. We had the best time swimming, fishing, canoeing and going to matinee movies. I also did a business plan to start a parenting consulting business to conduct parenting workshops. It was called Child Awareness and Resources for Encouragement Services (CARES). I had developed a series of parenting workshops that I facilitated for community organizations. Business was slow initially, so I worked at the Hilton.

After the Sugar Bowl game in 2000, Michael earned the Excellence in Sports Performance Yearly Award (ESPY) for the College Athlete of the Year. I was so excited and proud of his accomplishments. As a Hilton employee, I received a free birthday dinner at the restaurant of my choice. When I found out the ESPY Awards ceremony would be coming on television that day, I informed my managers that I wanted to use my birthday dinner certificate in the hotel's sports bar to watch my nephew win his award!!! All of the ten television sets were tuned in to the ESPY's. My children and I enjoyed a great meal as we watched him accept this then unimaginable award!!

Michael looked sharp on television. He walked out proudly in his fancy black tuxedo. I announced to everyone in the restaurant, "That's my nephew!" Some people looked at me as if to say, "Yeah right!" in the same manner they did when Michael and the Hokies came to the hotel for the Sugar Bowl. At that time, when I saw the coaches walking down the hall, I ran up to them and said, "Hello, how are ya'll doing? I'm Michael Vick's aunt!" They looked at me and said, "Yeah, o.k. You know everybody is related to him now." After I kept telling them personal information like, his Mom is my sister, they realized that I did look like Brenda. Deep inside, I don't think they believed me until my sister Brenda arrived.

Oogie arrived in New Orleans before his mother, Brenda did. I couldn't wait to see him. I had a co-worker in the business center to make a large sign that read, "My nephew is VT quarterback Michael Vick!!!!" I worked in a small office on the first floor of the Hilton Hotel and we had a small sign on the entry door, "The Training Department." I kept the sign in there until the day he arrived. I had already told people who worked around me, Patty, Alvina, Keirston, Laurie and Gretchen that he was my nephew. Everybody was waiting for the bus to arrive. Oogie had told some of the reporters that his aunt lived in New Orleans and several of them had already called the hotel for me to render comments. They wanted to know how I felt about him being a standout college athlete. It was exciting to be associated with one of the most talked about people in college football history.

Alvina and Patty went with me to the Hilton parking lot after security called our office to say the Virginia Tech team had arrived. I went out with my huge sign. The large white 50 passenger bus came to a halt. I kept looking through the windows to see when Oogie was coming off of the bus. He was one of the last ones to get off the bus, but I could see him smiling through the smoked glass window.

"Oogie!" I screamed as we hugged and kissed each other.
"Hey Aunt Tina!" he replied.

I couldn't believe he was in the "504," the New Orleans' area code, which many people used to refer to the city. "I can't believe you are here!" I said. "These are my bosses, Patty and Alvina."

"Hello Michael!" said Alvina as she shook his hand. "Hey Michael, nice to meet you! I'm Patty. We are going to show you to the floor where the rest of the team is going to stay," Patty said. "I am glad you are staying at the New Orleans Riverside hotel.

"Aunt Tina, I am going to get situated in my room and I will call you, after we finish practicing, to come see you tonight," Michael informed me.

"Okay, I get off this evening at 5:30 and I'll be heading to pick Felix and Tee up to take them home," I told him.

After I got home, I called Momma to let her know Oogie had made it to New Orleans. She was glad because she worried about all of us as we traveled. We waited for Oogie to call to get picked up. After it kept getting later, I gave him a call.

"Oogie are you still coming?" I asked.

"Yeah, yeah, I'm coming. We just stopped out here in the French Quarter for a few minutes after practice," he said.

"Well, be careful and don't let the strippers get you," I told him laughing.

"Oh naw, naw," he said.

I never did hear from Oogie that night because he was enjoying the French Quarter with the rest of the team. I had a feeling that those strippers from that strip joint with the fake women's legs swinging out of the window had convinced him that was the place to be. After he didn't show up, I knew he enjoyed the French Quarter's fun and madness. I know from experience it is hard to resist the New Orleans' French Quarter.

My sister Brenda kept called constantly to let me know the dates the family would be traveling to New Orleans. This would be Brenda's first time visiting me since I had moved to New Orleans in 1992.

"What flight will you be on Brenda, so I can make sure I am at the airport?" I asked.

"We don't know yet. We are trying to get everything together," she replied

"Well, let me know if you and Pickle (Brenda's husband) want to stay with me because I am close to the Superdome," I informed her.

"I will let you know as we make arrangements," Brenda said.

I couldn't wait to see my sister because I had not seen her since my summer vacation when I had gone home to visit. I was excited that she was on her way to see me!

It was the year before I planned to get married. I was elated about the upcoming wedding. Brenda and I talked a lot because we were very close. She listened to me discuss my wedding plans. I thought she would be happy about the wedding. Brenda was already married. She and my brother in law had some good times, but also a lot of rocky times. Brenda kept asking, "Tina, are you sure? Are you really sure you want to get married? You better think about it, because the grass looks greener on the other side. I am telling you Tina, the grass looks greener on the other side." Well, I took Brenda's advice, and I watched how things were going in my relationship over the next two months with my then fiancé. Things took a turn for the worst, and the marriage did not happen.

I could hardly work the day my family was scheduled to arrive. I was anxious about seeing my sister, her husband, my brother Casey and his family. Once they arrived, we roamed around the French Quarter. There were hundreds of thousands of people there from the Virginia Tech family. Many fans wore burgundy and orange shirts or jerseys representing the Hokies. The crowd was shoulder to shoulder as if it were time for the biggest New Orleans festival, Mardi Gras. There were layers of people of all colors. Pickle, my sister's husband really enjoyed himself. He was on cloud nine when people kept mistaking him for his son, Michael. "Ha! Ha! Ha! NO, I'm not Michael Vick, I'm his Dad, but thanks anyway for the compliment!" he laughed. Brenda couldn't stop teasing Pickle about this as she stated with a surprising tone, "I can't believe these people cannot tell you look older than Michael Vick!"

The day before the game, I took Michael around to meet my friends in the Hilton Hotel business center. The front of the business center was all glass, so guests could see inside the business center without coming inside. When Michael and I came out of the side office to leave, hundreds of Hokie fans had seen him and surrounded the entire business center. We could not get out! They held footballs and pictures of Michael and wanted his autograph.

"Oogie, how in the world do those people know you?" I asked.

"That's how it is, Aunt Tina, everywhere I go."

"I can't believe people know how you look under that helmet. I watch some football, but I wouldn't know any of those players if they didn't have their uniforms on to show what number they were," I told him.

Jackie, who was working in the business office, then said, "We are going to have to take him through the back of the hotel."

It was unbelievable! The fans would not let us out of the door. Oogie and I could not stop laughing. He had gotten used to it, but I was astonished about the crowds' reaction to my nephew.

It was Sugarbowl night. And Michael and the Hokies were ready. Michael fought his hardest to win for the Hokies. He was excited to play and gave the game everything he had. Reporters for the local news stations were calling me before the game. They wanted to know my opinion about my nephew and one newspaper, *The Times-Picayune* asked me to volunteer to connect a heart monitoring device to check my emotional heart levels the evening of the game. I agreed to do it and the next day, they had one of the craziest-looking pictures of me in the newspaper. I looked as if I escaped out of an insane asylum. The game was so intense. I carried my sign, "My Nephew is Michael Vick." He had much support from his family.

The Virginia Tech Hokies vs. Florida State Seminoles Sugar Bowl game was filled with big scoring plays and momentum swings. The Seminoles raced to a 28-7 lead; the Hokies came back to lead

29-28 late in the third quarter as a result of some sensational plays by Michael. He threw for 225 yards, made one touchdown, and ran for 97 yards and scored another touchdown. However, the Seminoles pulled away in the final quarter to win the Sugar Bowl. The loss ended the Hokies' dream season and the bid for its first national title in the 107 years of the team's existence. The USA today sports coverage of the Sugar Bowl spoke highly of my nephew stating, "Vick was valiant in defeat. The 19-year-old left-hander overcame a lost fumble near the Seminoles' goal line on the opening drive and led the Hokies back from a 21-point deficit to a 29-28 lead with 2:13 left in the third quarter." Michael fought his hardest and I was proud of his performance. I was the proud aunt still walking around with my sign, "My nephew is Michael Vick." I didn't care if the Hokies lost; they played a great game. Although they lost the Sugar Bowl, Michael's fight to win brought national attention to this new kid on the block from humble beginnings in Newport News, Virginia. After the Sugar Bowl, the media gave Michael several names, "Mr. Electrifying," "The Prince of the College Football" and the funniest one, which I loved the most, "Houdini."

Paul Buckley, who was the general manager of the Hilton at the time, gave the Hokies football team a special plaque from the Hilton family because the team was so well-behaved. We organized a special presentation for the entire Hokie team. Everyone was proud of the Hokies.

Michael had another good year with the Hokies in 1999. He made amazing plays and moves on the field. He broke the records of previous quarterbacks and had another winning season. His ability to dodge his opponents and make rifle like passes let the crowd know he was not your average player. Oogie also broke traditions by being a running quarterback who refused to stay in the pocket if he knew he could make a play. Little did we know that his multidimensional playing style would also bring a new and exciting approach to the NFL quarterback position.

After having one more great season, Michael decided to leave Virginia Tech and enter the pros. The night before he made the announcement, cameras were everywhere. It was a media circus, which included the large, sky-rocketing satellites from all of the local stations, Channel 3, 10 and 13 News, as well as ESPN. I saw the last technician leave Hampton Avenue at midnight. My children and I were up late because of the excitement of Oogie's announcement.

The next morning, Momma was there sitting with her head held high and looking proud of the young man she helped to raise. The Hokies Coach Frank Beamer was very emotional when Michael decided to leave. "In all of my years, I ain't never seen no white man cry over no black man before," Momma observed. "Frank Beamer was over there crying, or I guess I should say bawling, like Oogie was one of his children," Momma added.

Michael making his big announcement

CHAPTER SEVEN

THE NFL DRAFT

It felt like a dream. A member of the Vick Family was being drafted to play professionally in the National Football League (NFL). Witnessing the first person in our family to go pro was indeed a miracle. Michael was finishing up his third year at Virginia Tech and Blacksburg, Virginia was "Michael Vick" crazy. He had taken the Virginia Tech Hokies to an entirely different level. The stadiums were packed with more people than ever before.

His coach Frank Beamer and the Hokies team were enjoying the winning seasons and the notoriety of the media. I can honestly say that Coach Beamer and his team of professionals really cared about the young men they coached. In their arena, there were no "I's", only the team. Coach Beamer stayed grounded in all of the hoopla and kept his eyes focused on taking it game by game. He never took any game for granted.

Michael was dubbed as college football's most exciting player, and that he was!! When we went to the games, we just couldn't sit down. On several plays, the crowd would think the play was over, and skillfully, Michael would have conducted a magical move to escape his opponents. The flips into the end zones were show-stopping. It was amazing to see him in action!! It was never a dull moment when he was on the field! I have to say, whether he was my nephew or not, he was the most exciting player to watch in college football.

On January 11th, 2001, the day after my momma's birthday, Michael announced his football future. He made his announcement in a crowded gym at the Boys and Girls Club. "This has been one of the hardest decisions I've ever had to make in my life. I've decided to leave Virginia Tech . . . ," Before Michael could finish, his words were drowned by all the applause and cheers.

Almost all of the family was there. He made that announcement at approximately ten that morning, but I had been teary-eyed since about eight that morning. I lived across the street from the Boys and Girls Club, and I watched as family and friends gathered in the club to hear this important announcement. I cried primarily because Michael's success just blind-sided me. I never imagined him going to the NFL.

The thought did cross my mind when he was nominated in 1999 for the Heisman Trophy. Michael finished third in the balloting for the prestigious award. He received the highest number of votes for a freshman. All of us were excited as Michael and his mother, Brenda prepared to go to New York for the ceremony.

There are many parents who make plans for their child's future early on. They would force the child to go to practice, then even have drills for them to do as soon as they got home. The parents' main focus is having the child succeed in professional athletics. However, Brenda was the type of parent who never made Oogie go to practice. She wasn't nagging Oogie about playing football so he could make a better life for her; she just knew her son enjoyed playing. As a Mother, she showed her support for her child by going to the games, but never made it about her. Instead, Brenda allowed Michael and Marcus to enjoy being children and doing what they liked best, playing football. As part of his announcement, Michael said, "It's been my dream to play in the NFL ever since I've been a young boy watching football." Michael enjoyed playing football, and from his dedication to practice and studying the game, he was now making his dream a reality.

The NFL conversations about his prospect of being drafted began in 2000. VA Tech Coach Frank Beamer and several members of his staff flew to Newport News, Virginia during the last three months to spend several hours with Michael. They arranged for Michael to speak with several NFL quarterbacks who remained in school four years.

I had the privilege to be with Michael when he met with the high profile agent, Leigh Steinberg. The agent drove a classy, black Lincoln town car that looked like money. All of us were very nervous because no one had gone through this before, nor did we even know anybody to get advice from who had experienced this. We went to an attorney's office where Mr. Steinberg discussed the different options for Michael. He let us know it was an excellent chance that Michael would get drafted because so many teams had been watching him, not only while he was playing at the games, but also studying his plays on tape. Everyone kept saying it looked as if he would qualify for the first through the fifth pick, which was huge for someone who had not finished college. Not only that, they made it clear that if Michael declared that he wanted to forego college and participate in the draft, if he were not selected, he could not return to VA Tech to play football.

My sister and I were extremely nervous. I asked a lot of questions because I was nervous for my nephew since this was a tough decision! I asked the agent how sure was he about Michael actually being drafted as one of the top five of the picks. I have to admit that they were extremely confident. They were experienced and knew what the coaches were looking for when recruiting. Even with the information they presented, I still wasn't convinced.

As we continued to talk, there was a knock at the door. Mr. Steinberg's assistant stood up to open the door. When they opened it, Michael's eyes lit up and he smiled from ear to ear. The gentleman came in and shook our hands. As he shook Michael's hand, I heard Oogie say, "Hello, Steve McNair, I watched you as a young boy; man I looked up to you, and I wanted to be just like you!" Well, if Oogie's eyes lit up, I figured mine should too. I didn't know who the man was because I still couldn't figure out how football fans know who the players were without their uniforms. Brenda was sitting beside Oogie smiling.

Steve McNair was nicknamed "Air McNair" and played college football at Alcorn State in Mississippi, where he was the top player in the NCAA Division I-AA. He was a tall, very handsome man with a light, caramel-colored complexion. His stomach was flat as a washboard. He played in the NFL, first as quarterback with the Houston Oilers, then the Tennessee Titans and later the Baltimore Ravens. Steve allowed Mike to tell him how he felt about the entire ordeal. They also had dialogue about playing football, the draft, and leaving college early. Steve made it very clear that it would have to be Michael's decision. He said, "This is an opportunity of a lifetime. You are an amazing athlete. I've watched you and I think you should really consider taking this opportunity." We sat in the room a few minutes with him, and then we got a phone call from Donovan McNabb.

Donovan McNabb was the quarterback for the Philadelphia Eagles. He called to offer his support and comments about Michael's decision. Donovan encouraged Michael to take this opportunity because it doesn't happen to a lot of people. I still wasn't convinced someone was telling all of these guys to say this. "What if Michael left Virginia Tech and no one called him?" I kept thinking. I was hoping everyone in the room could see the concern on my face.

While Donovan was finishing up his conversation, a tall, dark muscular man came through the door. He was very soft spoken as he acknowledged all of us. "Hi, I'm Bruce Smith." He was Bruce Smith who played with the Washington Redskins. He came in very serious. He looked right at Michael and listened to the ending of Donovan's conversation. Bruce had such a presence. He was handsome and tall, and in good physical shape. His biceps were bulging through his short sleeved shirt. Bruce made eye contact with all of us in the room. "Alright, thanks Donovan, I really appreciate the advice, man," Michael said. "O.k. Michael, let me know how it goes," Donovan replied as they finished the call.

Because Bruce Smith was serious, his input made me feel much better. He was from the Hampton Roads Area and had also attended Virginia Tech. At Tech, he was the most honored player in the history of the Hokie nation. He went on to the NFL, first as a defensive lineman for the Buffalo Bills and then to the Washington

Redskins. His nickname was "The Sack Man" because he was the leader in tackles and sacks of quarterbacks.

Bruce was knowledgeable about the NFL. He looked Michael in the eyes, pointed his finger and said, "Michael, you have exceptional athletic ability. If you were any other athlete, I would tell you to finish college, but with your God-given athletic ability, you need to go." Since Bruce was in the football league and knew what to expect, we were reassured that Oogie would make the right decision. "Well, that's it then!" I thought. I don't need to ask any more questions. Oogie has always been very soft-spoken. He quietly responded, "Thank you Bruce. I will think about what you have told me, and I appreciate you coming to talk to me about this tough decision." Bruce listened to our concerns. After the meeting, we all shook hands and left the conference room.

The newspaper headlines read "Michael Vick Enters NFL Draft." It was all over the local and national news. What an exciting time for the Vick Family!! Our family member was actually going to the professional football league!! When I called my sister Diane, she was crying with excitement. "Diane can you believe this?" I asked as I stretched out to relax on my sofa. "Oh man, I feel like this is a dream!" she screamed.

For the first month or so the "dream" feeling remained in our hearts and minds. Then came reality all of a sudden the Vick Family became part of business plans, creating fan clubs, and working to help Michael once he got to the NFL. The next few months, the agents began taking over and having a stronger influence over Michael. There was less influence by family members. Once the agents took over, our enthusiasm became bittersweet. They advised Michael about the finances and investments. All of the business slowly went to people who were friends with the agents. And all of this started before he had even signed with a team.

All of this opened my eyes to an entirely new world. In this world the agents come into the lives of these young men, who are mostly African-American players from very low socio-economic backgrounds and know very little about money and investments. Imagine coming from that background and meeting these agents who are negotiating multi-million dollar deals. The agents who traditionally seek the players become the ones players trust. Unfortunately, they are not always trustworthy.

While finishing this chapter, I was watching the Wendy Williams show. She was showing a clip of the NFL player Vince Young, who came into the league after Michael Vick. Young was drafted in 2006 with the Tennessee Titans as a quarterback. The story was of Young's lavish spending. According to reports, he had gone through $29 million from eating out, spending money on friends and falling victim to corrupt financial advisors who had taken his money.

Many of these young players spend millions of dollars on their friends and know very little financially. Since most of the players come from poor neighborhoods, it is unbelievable that most of them don't use their money to make an economic impact in their own communities. When a person has been poor and not accustomed to millions of dollars, he or she has to make it a conscious effort to develop his or her financial mind.

When I began selling real estate, I knew that at 40 years old, I was way behind in my knowledge of financial literacy. I took several classes on managing money and building credit. I even read books on real estate and real estate investments to create a better economic situation for myself. These players have to do the same thing, increase their knowledge of business and finances. If they hire financial advisors, they must use people who are trustworthy.

I remained nervous about Michael deciding to leave Virginia Tech to enter the draft. I hadn't seen anything in writing officially stating, if he didn't go back to college, he would definitely have a spot as one of the draft picks. Michael said it was a chance he would go to San Diego, California. Brenda and I kept saying that was too far. A few days later, there was some talk about the Atlanta Falcons football team located in Atlanta, Georgia. Everybody was glad to hear that news because the City of Atlanta was much closer to Virginia. The agents told Michael, based on their calculations from NFL coaches and Michael's performance at the NFL Combine, his chances were great. It looked as if Michael would be selected anywhere from the first round of the draft pick to the fifth. I was not a football fanatic and I knew nothing about this draft day language. However, I knew the person to call was my brother, Casey. He loved sports, especially football, and would know everything that was going on.

"Hey Casey, how are you doing?"

"Good, just in this apartment getting it painted," he said.

"I was calling you to talk about what's going on with Oogie and this draft thing. Does it seem like he is getting a good deal?" I asked nervously.

"Yeah, Tina. From what I can see, if Oogie is able to be picked from the first to fifth in the draft, any one of those positions would be good," Casey informed me.

"I just want to make sure that these people know what they are doing and Oogie won't get screwed over," I said.

"He'll be alright! Casey assured me. I'm sure they know what they are doing."

"Oh that's good and it makes me feel a whole lot better. Thanks Casey."

Since Casey knew everything about football, I felt confident that if it was alright with him—it was alright with me. After talking to him, I felt more relaxed about the situation.

As the actual day of the draft became closer, Brenda made preparations for family members who wanted to fly to New York to attend the draft day ceremony. She booked flights for me and my children. We really wanted Momma to go, but she had a "phobia about traveling" as she called it. Momma told us she would just watch it on television.

When we arrived in New York, Brenda, and her daughters, Niki and Courtney were already there. We stayed at The W Hotel on

Madison Avenue. We took a shuttle from LaGuardia International Airport to the hotel. When we arrived, Michael was waiting for us in the hotel lobby.

"Hey Aunt Tina, did ya'll have a good flight?" he asked as he greeted us.
"Yes, it was good and it didn't take long for us to get here," I informed Michael.
"This is a really nice hotel Ook!" Tee said.
"Yeah it is nice; I'm just glad you could make it, he said. Now, go ahead and check-in at the front desk."

The W Hotel was nice. The lobby had large bowls of green apples for all of the hotel guests. Niki and Tee kept getting the apples, eating them, and taking several to their room. There was a round bar in the far left corner of the lobby where Tee, Marcus, and his girlfriend, Keyla were hanging out. After taking our luggage upstairs, we headed back down to the lobby. When we got downstairs, all of Oogie's friends from the neighborhood were there. He had invited his entire "hood" entourage to the draft. Everyone enjoyed themselves riding out on the town in a limousine.

Draft day finally came. There was excitement everywhere! All of our family members were all dressed up. There were the other top picks for the draft there along with their family members who were dressed up as well. Everyone was waiting in the hotel lobby. I went over to congratulate the Tomlinson Family. I went over to the mother because I loved her son's name, Ladainian Tomlinson. He was a quarterback from Texas Christian University. On that day he was chosen as the fifth overall draft pick by the San Diego Chargers. This day would impact the life of each family present in the lobby. The multi-million dollar contract deals would make improvements to each recruits entire family. Our family stood outside of the hotel on Madison Avenue to take pictures before we left for the event. All of the Vick's Family men looked so handsome. They even had that Vick swagger. All of us looked stunning as we took picture after picture. The draft negotiations had been taking place up to that very day, which transferred Michael from fifth place to potentially first place in the draft pick. We were all extremely proud of Oogie. He handled all of his success very well.

The shuttle arrived to take us to the program at the Madison Square Garden Center. I had no clue as of the agenda for the entire day. However, it was another day media circus! Crews from ESPN, ABC, NBC, and various television stations were outside as special guests entered into the building. Since there were special seating arrangements, the agent had given us badges. When we went in, the ushers allowed Brenda and her children to go backstage and the other Vick Family members went into a special seating area.

Then, the NFL commissioner welcomed everyone. He began to announce the top ten draft picks. "Announcing the Number One draft pick . . . from Virginia Tech in Blacksburg, Virginia, Michael Vick, who will be the quarterback for the Atlanta Falcons!" Michael and his immediate family, along with the agent, went on the stage. Michael had on the Falcons hat and displayed his new Falcons #1 jersey. Everyone was clapping and shedding tears of joy. It was an unbelievable part of our lives. The strength and hard work of the Vick Family lineage had paid off for my nephew, Michael Vick. He became the first African-American quarterback to be drafted as the number one overall pick in the history of the NFL.

Michael Vick in his Atlanta Falcons uniform

My nephew Greg Brooks opening the First Aaron Brooks
& Michael Vick All-star Weekend That's me, James "Pooh"
Johnson & Michael Vick

CHAPTER EIGHT

A NEW BEGINNING

I decided to return home from New Orleans, Louisiana because Momma's health was becoming a problem. She began having problems with her heart and had "angioplasty" surgery. The last time I had come home to visit, she had also been diagnosed with diabetes.

Two days before I left from my last visit, Momma was in her bedroom asleep. Normally, she got up early around 6:00 in the morning. This particular morning, I got up before she did, around 7:00. I kept moving around the house and realized that Momma still had not awakened. At approximately 7:30 in the morning, she was still not awake and I had a feeling something was wrong. So, I went into her bedroom and tapped her arm. Her entire arm slumped to the floor. I started screaming, "Momma! Ma! I gotta call an ambulance!" I screamed, "My Momma! My Momma!" as I rushed to find the phone. I called the ambulance and kept shaking my momma until the ambulance came. Her eyes opened, but not for long. Every time they opened, they rolled around in her head.

At this point, Momma had moved to Riverland Apartments in Newport News. The ambulance didn't take long to arrive at all. I opened the door and frantically told the paramedics what happened. I informed them that she was a diabetic. The paramedic pulled out some glucose, packaged in a small, white tube and squeezed it in Momma's mouth. They connected her to all types of tubes to check her vital signs. She was still breathing.

"Her pressure is low," the paramedic said.
"Please help my Momma." I begged in desperation.
"We're doing all we can miss." As soon as he said this, Momma began opening her eyes and trying to say some words.

"Lord, what are the paramedics in here for?" she asked as she tried to regain her strength. "Ma, you wouldn't wake up and your body was lifeless," I told her.

"What! My sugar count must have been extremely low. I didn't eat enough last night."

"Well, we are going to stay here for a few minutes to make sure everything is alright. Your blood sugar level needs to continue to go up. If not, we'll have to take you to the hospital."

"The hospital, no I'm not going to no hospital. I'll be just fine right here," she said.

Momma's blood sugar level kept going up. I went in the kitchen to make her a peanut butter and jelly sandwich on wheat bread. She ate some of it, but she was still too weak to finish it. The paramedics took one more reading and everything checked out alright.

"Thank you for helping us." I stated to the paramedics.
"Not a problem ma'am. That's what we're here for."

When they left I was still afraid. I immediately called my relatives to let them know what happened. This incident made me think long and hard on my way back to New Orleans. My mother needed me because she had gotten old. She had taken care of all of us. I knew it was time for me to come back home.

I rented a duplex, also located in Newport News, on Hampton Avenue when I returned home. All of my life I had always rented places to live. I grew up in a time when it was uncommon for single women to purchase homes. I always thought that when I married my husband and I would buy a house together. Once I got in my 40's and started selling real estate, I realized it was a good chance I was not getting married. I would have to make the move on my own. Eagerly, I began looking to buy my very first house.

I just firmly believe that if we as a black community want others to invest in our communities, we should do likewise. Just like there are some whites who don't want to live around me because of my race, I definitely don't want to live around anyone with that type of attitude. Even though I have many friends who are white, there are still a few white people who don't want blacks as their neighbors. I didn't want to move anywhere I wasn't welcomed. I was very comfortable living in my own community.

I searched for some time until I found a vacant piece of land located in Newport News on Ivy Avenue. The dimensions were perfect and I was able to get my house built. I was ecstatic when I wrote up my contract with the builder, Dennis Favors with Faden Contracting, Incorporated, who had helped me build and renovate other properties in the South District. He was able to begin on my home right away.

My house was completed in the hot summer month of July. It consisted of four bedrooms, with two and a half baths. I loved my nice bedroom on the first floor and my children's bedrooms were upstairs. One bedroom I used for office space. Dennis allowed me to select a lovely gray brick for the front of the house and a light gray for the siding to go around the whole house. The house had an open floor plan, which I had described to Dennis and he made it a reality.

The housewarming was the best housewarming ever! It started at approximately 5:00 in the evening and lasted until. It was such a celebration for me.

"I want this housewarming to be a great event!" I told my daughter, Teunsha.
"Ma, you should have it on a Friday."
"Yes, what a great idea! We can start early. We can have all of the formalities at the beginning and then have drinks and stuff for the real party, huh Tee?" I asked.
"Yes, Friday August 12ᵗʰ (2005) is the best date."

Tee was working in Anne Arundale County, Maryland at the time, as a catering manager for one of the hotels. My baby girl had grown up to be such a professional. She helped me with the menu in the evening when she finished working. We would discuss by phone our plans.

"I want to have a variety of foods, especially some of my New Orleans specialties," I told her.

"Yeah, Ma, I think you should cook some red beans and rice and jambalaya. Then we can have punch and various wines for refreshments," she said.

"I want to have some pigs' feet. I know the right person to call to cook them for the housewarming."

I immediately hung up the phone with my daughter to make that phone call. "Hello Faye," I said loudly when she answered the phone. "My housewarming is Friday, August 12th and I want to see if you can make some pigs' feet for me?"

"Sure Tina," Faye said. "If I have enough time, I'll bring the pigs' feet and some macaroni and cheese too," she added.

"Thanks a bunch, girl, because you know everybody loves your pigs' feet! What time do you think you and Bruce will come over?" I asked her.

"I'll bring the food at about 3 o'clock and we will come over about 7 o'clock.

Faye Rose was a bus driver with Newport News Public Schools (NNPS). She had gotten a promotion to the NNPS bus administration office. I helped Faye and her husband Bruce find their first house when they moved to 23rd Street in Newport News. When she would have functions at her job, everyone loved her pigs' feet and her macaroni and cheese! My sister Diane would say," Faye makes the best macaroni and cheese, with a whole lot of cheddar cheese and she sprinkles freshly cooked bacon on top of it."

The day came for the housewarming and everything was in place. We had a nice program. My mom usually didn't go anywhere, but I was glad she decided to come out. "I want to welcome all of you and thank you for your support of this great accomplishment in my life," I announced. "Now, we will have a prayer by Alvin

Armstead." Alvin worked with me as the construction manager for our program. He was also a youth minister at Gethsemane Baptist Church. Alvin did a heartfelt prayer and blessed the food. Everyone loved my Louisiana cuisine and the soul food. We even had a few finger sandwiches, platters of cheese, fruits and vegetables.

Bob Ayers came to my housewarming. We had kept in touch over the years because he was a great mentor. He now was the executive director of the Office of Human Affairs and I worked for him.

"Hey Tina, can you put me one of those pigs' feet in this bowl?" Bob asked.

"Okay, do you want me to fix you a bowl of red beans and rice too?" I asked.

"Yes, of course, put me some right in this same bowl," he said. He revealed the next week when we were back at work, "Yeah, Tina after you fixed my bowl of beans, I went out the back door on the porch and I put a hurting on that food!" he said laughing. "It was delicious!"

At the housewarming, we had lots of music and games. I even gave door prizes too. Throughout the night, we had over a hundred people to come through the doors of my beautiful home. Before the last guests left, Carol McIntosh Totten, who loves to clean, had washed all the dishes and tidied up my kitchen. Carol was always talking smart to people and kept the crowd laughing. When the last guest did leave, which was about 3:00 in the morning, I laid my head on my pillow and whispered, "Thank you Lord for this accomplishment—owning my own home. This was my American dream come true."

A few years later, I started my own real estate company. Karen Ivey, one of my friends, became an agent with my company, Tina L. Vick Realty and Development, LLC. I had met Karen when we served on the Social Services Board for our city. She called me one day and told me she had heard that the vice mayor of the City of Newport News was not running for another term. She asked if I was interested. It was February of 2008. No one in my family had ever been in politics so I told her I had to think about it.

I appreciated her thinking about me for the opportunity. Several other people called to ask me to consider running for office. I called the Office of the Vice Mayor to personally speak with him regarding if he was not running for another term. I knew that the vice mayor had a lot of support from the community and out of respect, I would not run for the seat if he was considering re-election.

"Hello Vice Mayor," I said through the phone.
"This is Tina Vick."
"Hello, Tina. How are you doing?" he asked.
"I'm fine. Several people have called me about running for the seat you are vacating," I said to him. "But I do not want to run, if you are still interested. Is it true you are not running for re-election?"
He paused and said, "I am thinking about not seeking re-election."
"Well, please let me know if you are not running for office, because I would like to consider myself a candidate for the south district seat," I informed him.

After our conversation, I went to several people in the community to let them know I wanted to run for the Newport News City Council. I stopped to talk to Mrs. Vinson to tell her about my intentions to run for office. She always sat on her front porch.

"Hello, Mrs. Vinson. How are you today?" I asked.
"Fine Tina. It's good to see you," she said smiling.
"I stopped by to ask for your support. I am thinking about running for a seat on the Newport News City Council."
"Now you know you have my support. It will be the first time I have voted for anybody locally," she said.
"Oh Mrs. Vinson, I am deeply honored! Your support means a lot to me."

Mrs. Vinson asked, "So, are you gonna run your election under another name?" (She was referring to the Michael Vick dogfighting saga, which was happening at the time. Mrs. Vinson felt like people would not vote for me because of it.)

"No, I am running under my own name," I informed her.
"Oh really? Well Tina, I hope things work in your favor."
"Mrs. Vinson, I do too, and I really appreciate your support."
Mrs. Vinson was my best friend, Gwen Andrews' mother. Gwen and I had known each other since seventh grade at Dunbar-Erwin Elementary School.

After my conversation with Mrs. Vinson, I felt like Tina Turner in the movie, *What's Love Got To Do With It?* In the movie, when Tina told the lawyers during her divorce hearing from her husband, Ike, "Yeah, you can give him all the rest of that other stuff, but just give me my name. I have worked too hard for him to take that." That's right! I was running in the election on my own name, **TINA L. VICK**, despite all the impending matters concerning my nephew. I had built a life for myself and people would understand.

As a native of the City of Newport News, I always loved the city and the community. As a community activist, I always advocated in helping to solve many of my community's issues and was not afraid of the challenges. Since I never received a call back from the vice-mayor, I decided to proceed in running for a seat on the Newport News City Council. Therefore, I took the ball and ran with it! The day came for me to submit all of my information and make my declaration of candidacy to the voter registrar's office. I also submitted a press release to *The Daily Press*, the local newspaper. The reporter who received my press release called me to verify all of my information.

The reporter then asked me one thing that was not on my press release, "Are you Michael Vick's auntie?"

"Yes, I am," I boldly replied.
"Are you, really?" the reporter questioned.

From the entire phone conversation that ironically seemed to be the only thing about me that sparked the reporter's interest.

When the newspaper came out the next day with the city council contenders throughout the city, it listed my two opponents' names first and mine last. My name was shown last because the reporter listed the names alphabetically (according to our last names). The listing had shown my two opponents' names, their professions and activities. However, for me, it read, "For the south district seat, real estate agent, Tina L. Vick, aunt of the suspended NFL Atlanta Falcons quarterback, Michael Vick." I was appalled and several looming thoughts began to run through my mind. Maybe I am being unrealistic and I should just drop out of the race? Would citizens, who were mad about the Michael Vick dogfighting scandal, tape pictures of pit bulls to my campaign yard signs? Would potential voters blame me for what my nephew allegedly did?

My heart sank, and for a few minutes I was skeptical. I quickly refocused as God put in my spirit, "Don't worry! The last shall be first and the first shall be last!!" I was immediately empowered and charged to run in the race for this election. This was my first time, but, worst case, I would have a great learning experience. I didn't want to come in second place, I wanted to win!

My team of supporters worked hard to defeat my opponents. My oldest nephew Greg was my campaign manager. He and his team devised a plan to win. We all hit the streets to hand out campaign literature. My daughter helped out all the time. She had already had my second grandson, Tyree, and he was about three months old. We had a joke in the campaign that his first words would be "safe, decent and affordable housing," which was part of my platform.

John Eley worked as the public relations expert. He made sure our campaign had plenty of fliers and our events were packed with supporters. We endured the forums and the debates. I had been working in the community and involved in housing developments, served on several boards, so I was already ahead of my opponents in knowledge about the district and our city.

The district I was striving to represent, I grew up in and knew not only the communities within it but also many of the people in that region. Many of my friends and other constituents were so glad to see someone from their own community running for office. I had a lot of people in the community supporting my campaign and efforts.

Carolyn Johnson volunteered to create fliers initially for the start of the campaign. She and I had begun investing in real estate together seven years earlier. Over the years, we had become friends. She was an attractive woman who was very petite. She loved creating documents on the computer. The Vick Team kept most of her ideas. Carolyn had created a nice picture with me standing in front of an American flag.

At the beginning of the campaign, we couldn't decide on the 2008 campaign slogan. "What about 'Out with the Old and in with the New,'" Carolyn suggested with a laugh.

"Mrs. Carolyn, you know that sounds crazy!" Tee said laughing. "Oh I know Ma, 'My Momma will Make a Difference!'" Tee suggested. "You should let me stand on stage with a picture of you, Ma," Tee laughed as she clapped her hands.

I do think she seriously wanted to use that slogan. However, I wanted a slogan that would describe my campaign goals. "I know, 'Working for the People,'" I said.

Carolyn questioned, "Doesn't someone already have 'Working for the People?'" Tee and I shrugged our shoulders indicating we didn't know. She then suggested, "What about 'Committed to Making a Difference!'"

"Yes, yes!!!" I agreed as I jumped up and down.

My daughter replied, "That's right, Ma, because our campaign will be committed to making a difference in our city and in the lives of citizens!"

Carolyn worked hard for the Vick Campaign and volunteered to work as my treasurer. It was a learning process, but she mastered it in a short time. We also learned how to raise money.

One of our biggest challenges was ordering the yard signs. We had no clue where we could get the signs printed. Carolyn asked her son, Tremaine and co-workers about the design. They put a nice palm card together along with the design for the yard signs. Carolyn let me review the design. It was creative and included all of the pertinent information. I told Carolyn to go ahead and order the signs from the printing company located in Norfolk, Virginia. We only had five more weeks before Election Day, which was on May 6th. After Carolyn had placed the order with the printers, it took them a week to get the 500 signs ready.

Once the signs were ready, we looked at them and discovered that we had forgotten to include the following disclosure statement on them: "By Authority of Tina L. Vick" or "Paid for by Friends of Tina L. Vick." A candidate without a disclosure statement on all of their distributed campaign materials would have imposed fines to pay. As a result of our oversight, we could not get a refund and I regrettably was left with five hundred wasted signs in my garage. Since the printing company took so long with our first order, we decided not to let them redo the signs. We immediately had to scramble to find another printing company that could expedite our order. At this point, our campaign time was down to approximately three weeks, and our time was running out fast. Fortunately, I knew George Wallace, a candidate running for the Hampton City Council, so I called him directly to find out what printing company he used. He informed me about an on-line printing company that could print the signs in one day and ship them for next day delivery. We contacted that on-line printing company to redo the signs and received our order the very next day. Thank God, everything worked out.

On the second Friday before Election Day, I woke up around 6 o'clock in the morning to go out to campaign at the Longshoremen Hall located in Newport News on the corner of 18th Street and Ivy Avenue. I stood outside, across from Zion Baptist Church, and waited for some of the longshoremen to come outside or drive up. I thought they would be outside, coming to the hall to pick up their paychecks. I stood outside for approximately thirty minutes, waiting for someone to come around. It was a ghost town all morning. The employees were enrolled in direct deposit due to technology and there were not that many employed as in the past.

I finally called my daughter and told her that no one was coming out. I wonder why no one was out there?" Teunsha shouted. "Well, times have changed and things are different in this community," I said. A lot of things candidates had to do before to get elected won't work in the new age of technology. Since it was early, I thought about going home to get some rest, but something told me to go and sit with Momma.

At this time, Momma lived in a quiet neighborhood in the Oyster Point area located in the central part of the City of Newport News. She just loved our city and if anyone even suggested moving anywhere else, she would remind them, "Joe brought me to Newport News, Virginia and I wanna stay right here in Newport News." I sat with Momma for at least three hours that day.

She kept looking at me and smiling, then she said, "Tina can you open up those blinds for me? I want some more sun to come in here." Momma loved to open her blinds early in the morning. I think that's why we were always happy. The sunlight, which increases the serotonin levels in your body, helped to keep our family happy. She always ensured that sunlight shined into our home no matter where we lived.

Momma and I loved watching the news and reading the paper. On that particular day, we watched *Good Morning America* because both of us absolutely loved Diane Sawyer. During the commercial breaks, we read the newspaper to find out the "local happenings" within our city and in the surrounding areas. As a candidate running for office, I needed to constantly stay abreast of the local and national news.

"Alright Momma, I'm getting ready to head to this interview," I told her and kissed her on the cheek.
"Oh, okay, Tina. You gotta work today?" Momma asked.

"Yes, Ma, that's why I'm leaving now," I informed her. Unfortunately, on that day, Momma had already asked me three times earlier if I had to work. I had told her yes three times.

During 2007, Momma's doctor diagnosed her with dementia, which is the beginning stage of Alzheimer's disease. In the prior few months, some of the things we told Momma, she would forget and keep asking the same questions again and again. I headed out the door, but Momma wanted me to throw some things away for her before I left.

As I was throwing the bags from her kitchen cabinet into the trash container, I said, "Momma, I don't know if I am gonna win this election because I have two opponents. I've been studying the issues and reading the newspaper every single day." Momma looked at me and started shaking her head and said, "Oh you gone win Tina, you are gone win!" Momma pointed her finger as she was talking to me "With all of those smart brains in your head, I know you gone win. I don't know where you got all those smart brains from, but you sure didn't get it from me," Momma said as she laughed.

I felt great as I left Momma's house because she was my biggest cheerleader. Many times in my professional life when I had major accomplishments in the community, I would sit with Momma and tell her about them. When I worked with Faden Contracting, Inc. to renovate and build new properties in the southeast section of the city, I was extremely proud of the homes Dennis and I produced. Even though the homes were for low to moderate income, we spiced the houses with brick fronts, real hardwood floors and jetted tubs. I was especially proud of finding people who only knew about renting apartments and public housing. I helped in training them in the home ownership process. There was no greater achievement for me than to see them buy their own home. Helping to transform their minds to start building wealth.

Momma would sit there and say "that's good," but I don't believe she had the faintest idea about what I was actually doing. I loved hearing my momma's voice, because she had a strong North

Carolina accent. When she spoke it sounded kinda like she sang when she talked. It would make me laugh, but it was also encouraging.

I campaigned continuously. Several of the previously elected officials did not support me in my first campaign. I eventually found out why.

A few days after my visit with Momma, I received a call from my oldest brother. He said, "Momma is on the sofa and she won't wake up."

I screamed at him, "Call the ambulance!" I jumped up and put my clothes on and headed to Riverside Hospital where we always took Momma for her medical emergencies. Momma gave birth to all of her children except for Joe Jr. at that hospital and we knew she would not have wanted us to take her anywhere else. My sister called before I left and informed me that she was on her way to the hospital to meet us. We waited in the hospital's family room until the doctor came out. "Well, your Mom has suffered a stroke," the doctor said. "She appears to have had a blood clot in her leg which caused a blockage. The blockage in her leg caused her to have the stroke."

As the doctor told us about the blood clot, my mind reminisced back to my last visit at Momma's house. If Momma didn't move around and do anything else, she would always get up to open the blinds to her patio door. I remembered from my last visit with Momma, that entire time she remained sitting on the sofa. She didn't even walk to the kitchen like she normally did. While I was there, she said to me, "Tina, can you get up and open up my blinds for me?" I began to wondering if she probably didn't get up because she was in pain and didn't want me to know.

They had put Momma in the Intensive Care Unit (ICU) located on the 4th floor of the hospital where she was connected to a respirator which made her breathe for a couple of days. I was scared to go in her hospital room alone, but I had to do it. It was sad to see my mother connected to that respirator. It caused her chest to rise every few seconds. Periodically, her eyes would just flash open and then immediately close, as if someone was trying to wake her up by sticking a needle in her. When she kept flashing her eyes open and closed, I felt like she sensed her family's presence and was giving us the signal, "I'm holding on ya'll. I'll be alright in a few days."

It was just awful watching Momma in her condition, laying in that hospital bed like that without being able to help her. Many of our friends and other family members slowly came to the ICU's family waiting room. The situation didn't look good.

Despite the family tragedy, I attended a few more forums, but didn't stay for the entire time. The doctors called the Vick Family in and informed us that Momma was pronounced dead on Friday, May 2, 2008. On Election Day, Tuesday, May 6th, I struggled to shake hands with my supporters in between my burst of tears. That night, we were having my mother's wake. I had cried so much during the day that my eyes were swollen. Well, the results were in for the election by the time our family and friends left the funeral home. Just as God promised, "the first shall be last and the last shall be first." It indeed happened. Our campaign had received the highest votes at 1778, and my opponent, who was listed first, came in last with a little over 500 votes. The other opponent came in second with approximately 900 votes. The words God had spoken to me had come to pass and I was clapping for joy! The Vick Campaign had just slaughtered our competitors and I was now the new Newport News City Council representative for Seat A for the South District! It was truly unbelievable!

Carolyn, my campaign treasurer called, "Tina, I heard our opponents say they had won the election. How much did they beat us by?" Carolyn asked nervously.

"Oh, they didn't beat us . . . we won by a long shot!" I informed her.

"What!?' Carolyn screamed.

"Yes, we slaughtered them!" I said to her again.

"Well, some lady at the poll said they won the election," she said.

"She must be thinking they won in her head because they sure did lose!" I said.

We both started laughing.

My daughter, Tee replied, "We blew them away, Ma!"

"I'm going home. I'm telling everybody thanks for helping out with the campaign, but there will not be a victory party because of my mother's passing," I informed her. "I will come over there for awhile tomorrow."

"Tina, girl, we did it, for your first campaign!" Carolyn screamed. "Yes!"

I replied, "I am so happy and thank you so much!"

The very next morning, after Election Day, the Vick Family prepared for Mother's funeral. The sadness and grief I felt in my body did not want to let me get up out of my bed. How do you go on when the woman who has been with you every single day of your life is no longer here? Our mother, Caletha Virginia Vick was no longer with the Vick Family. Her six children, with all of our accomplishments, couldn't understand this.

The Cooke Brothers Funeral Home, located in Newport News, was in charge of the funeral arrangements. They were professional and attended to our every need. My house was the point of contact for the gathering of all our family and friends.

Tamika Dawson, one of the first persons to arrive at my house, came by to express her sympathy to the Vick Family. She was one of the kids who lived in Newport News on Lassiter Drive, who had gotten into a physical fight with my nephew Oogie and niece Niki when they were younger. Momma would not let the thought of children fighting leave her mind. She was mad for years from this fight with the grandchildren whom she adored.

When Tamika knocked on my door, I let her in, but I was thinking, "What in the world?" I was talking to her, but I kept thinking, do you know how long my mother was mad at you because of what you did to Oogie and Niki? It gets worse. Oogie's Dad was extremely mad about the fight. He didn't want anyone picking on his children. He went to the Dawsons' apartment and took his bare hands and smashed half of their windows out in retaliation. All of us were standing in her yard fussing and cursing about a children's fight. Tamika was now all grown up and she came to pay her last respects to the family. I knew she had no clue Momma was still mad at her for fighting Oogie and Niki, some twenty years ago.

My daughter came over after the funeral. We were having a general conversation when she said, "I miss Grandma already."

"I do too and I hope nobody comes over here. I don't feel like having to entertain anyone because I am not feeling it." I said.

"It was a great homegoing service and lots of people came out to show their love. I still can't get over that man last week at the community center forum asking you do you really think you are going to win with all of the allegations against your nephew Michael Vick concerning the dogfighting situation?" Tee questioned.

"Yeah, he was rather nutty. I bet now he can clearly see I had nothing to do with that dogfighting matter. The citizens' votes showed they supported me. I want to do a great job and have a vision for making this area more functional," I said.

"You will, Momma I know you can do it," Tee said reassuringly.

I had my ideas about improving a portion of the City of Newport News' South District area which has suffered the most. Over 12% of the people within a section of that district were unemployed. Unfortunately, the majority of those individuals were black. For them, there was very little to no job training nor even connections to jobs. Much of the business in the city had moved northward. It was as if no one had any solutions to what could help this area improve.

Well, I was full of ideas and solutions to help improve the area. I wanted to give a better view to the families who were experiencing generational poverty and to let poor families know that you don't have to remain poor. Years before running for office, I began partnering with local churches to see if there were any men who were concerned about the numbers of young black males on the street corners playing dice and selling drugs. As I rode past some of the street corners where the young men would stand, I could see hopelessness and despair on their faces. I could tell they had no clue about the purpose they were to serve here on earth. Our area of Newport News was one with high levels of female headed households, which translated to irresponsible fathers.

I found it mind boggling to see that many ministers in the area were not even concerned. I thought the church involvement would work because the black men in the church, who were living right, could definitely mentor the young men on the street corners and help to transform their lives. From my experiences, most ministers just wanted people to come to their churches to give money to build mega churches. They were not concerned with going out to the streets to minister to the hearts and souls of the people. They were not interested in doing like Jesus did. They were comfortable staying confined within the walls of their church.

When I was with PCDC, the agency received a grant to start a deconstruction company. It was my responsibility to actually administer the grant projects. My first step was to find companies to employ adults between the ages of 18 to 24 and provide them with on-the-job training to deconstruct buildings. Deconstruction was a new concept, which was popular in places such as Pennsylvania and New Jersey. It involved a systematic way of taking a building apart. The materials i.e. bricks, windows, doors and molding were used for resale. Initially, we had a difficult time finding the buildings until we found a special project at Fort Monroe, Virginia.

The grant was specifically for low income areas and the benefit was to employ people. I didn't realize how much our community had changed. With that target population, it was very difficult to find young men who wanted to work every day. Almost every young man who came to apply had a felony. It was unbelievable! I kept wondering when did it became alright not to want to work? What happened to make people think it was acceptable to go to jail? The unemployment rate in southeast community was higher than the national average. Something had to be done. I just believed that if we had a job training facility with a connection to jobs, it would improve peoples' lives and make our neighborhood much better.

I personally had a meeting with a few city leaders and officials as well as some past representatives. To be quite honest, most of them didn't seem to care about the City of Newport News South District's population or the people located in its downtown area. During our meetings, several individuals even told me that downtown Newport News no longer existed within the South District area. Instead, the new downtown vicinity was located in the Oyster Point area of Newport News in a new development called "City Center." I politely informed them that myself and other citizens still lived downtown. I suggested they call the City Center area, our central business district because, like it or not, we were still in downtown Newport News. One man I met with spoke franticly as he hit the table with his fist, "We need to move our city hall building to the central part of the city." I took it as bullying. I definitely was not going to be bullied by anyone.

The table hitting seemed to be a common practice of most of these political bullies. However, I politely informed the individual that I would love to see who would be brave enough to do that, move our City Hall. I could not believe some of the things I heard. These negative comments about the people in the southeast community, including me, were made by business and community leaders. They had devised a plan which would leave the black people in the downtown area "to die." Nobody seemed to care. There was excuse after excuse about why things wouldn't work in our area, but I was not going to give up.

Unfortunately, I received very little support from community leaders about the job training center and other ideas I had to improve the housing situation. After the meeting with the last leader, which I call my final straw meeting, I began to figure out what was happening. In that meeting, he looked at me, looked at his nails, looked at me again and with a stern look said, "Tina, you know what they say about those people down there; they say, they don't need anything." I was appalled and, needless to say, extremely disappointed to hear this from him. I sat there in his office and didn't know what to say. "Well," I said, "I guess there are some people who feel like that."

After returning home from the meeting, I thought about what that "good ole system" had done. It had provided very little to no economic investments, poor housing conditions, no job training and no access to job opportunities. This troubled me. All of the things communities need to thrive and people need to live were virtually cut off. People were living in an area that was deprived of a connection to a better future. Thousands of lives were lost and in disarray because of limited or no opportunities.

I thought about my nephew, Micheal Vick, receiving a 23 months sentence to prison for killing dogs. When these people had killed the lives of thousands of people. None of them went to jail, but were criminals. I was committed to making things better. I was distraught to know that there were so-called leaders who did not want to help others improve their living situation. Definitely not all of the business felt this way. There was a small gang of them, which my friends and I call the "business thugs."

These "business thugs" despised minorities and were disgusted about women being in public office. They didn't believe in justice for all. That's the reason why some of the leaders and ministers initially did not support me. With that group, if they could not control your thinking and your votes, they would not support you.

It just so happened that when I was elected, there was another female candidate running for the Newport News City Council seat for the Central District area who had stomped five of her opponents on her way to victory—Dr. Patricia Woodbury. There were already two women on the Newport News City Council, but once Dr. Woodbury and I won, that made the total four. For the first time ever, this was the most women at one time represented on council. With a seven member council, four votes meant the majority. We were not only four women; we were four smart women who studied the issues. We were confident and we had the citizens' of Newport News best interest at heart.

The "good ole boy system" was not pleased with women talking and expressing ideas of what was working in our city and what needed to be improved. They were upset, because I was vocal about solutions needed in the South District on joblessness, crime, and inadequate housing. Also, I questioned the unnoticed code violations and lack of economic investment. When I began to bring this to everyone's attention, several of the establishment set up meetings with me. They all warned, "Tina you might not want to say anything about the problems in your district because the next time you run for office, you might not get the financial support to get elected." I stopped one guy in the middle of his conversation as we were leaving a restaurant. "No, no, no, don't tell me that . . . let me tell you something. I am not going to be immobilized for the next four years, afraid about saying this or that," I further stated, "I will say in my heart what I think is right, and the people will decide in 2012 if they think I should be re-elected." He was dumbfounded and left me alone after that incident.

For the next four years though, with much resistance, council members voiced their opinions and shared ideas to improve the lives of the citizens throughout our entire city. It took all the strength I had to stand up to a system which secretly said, "All for the 1% and nothing for the people who just needed an opportunity." I refused to be a part of such a system.

CHAPTER NINE

THE DREADED REVELATION

My real estate career was very lucrative. The market was booming and I loved it! It was a time in real estate no one had ever experienced. There was an enormous number of buyers. When a listing agent put a house on the market, he or she could easily end up with ten to twenty contracts! People were buying like crazy! There were more agents in the business than ever before. Contractors were building houses wherever there was available land.

Mid-year 2007, I received my Real Estate Broker's License. I failed the Broker's test on my first try because I was so nervous! I told too many people when I was going to take the test. On that day, everyone began calling saying, "Good Luck! I know you can do it!" It made me more nervous. That's why I think I failed. The second time I went, I told everyone who usually calls me during the day that I was going to a meeting, which would last about two hours and I would call them when I finished. When I finished my last question, I clicked on the button denoting "Finish." I had passed the state and the national broker's test!!! I was now a real estate broker with John E. Wood Realty, Inc. and I was on "Cloud 9!"

After completing four courses for my broker's license and studying for the test, I was due for a much needed vacation. The first place in my mind was one of the cities I enjoyed living in the most . . . New Orleans, Louisiana. Boiled crawfish, fat boiled crabs and the shrimp and hot sausage po' boys were enough to make anybody want to live in New Orleans, not to mention the late nights on the Riverwalk and the carriage rides through the French Quarter. I called one of my best girlfriends, Andrea, and told her I needed a vacation. Andrea was very pretty and had a heavy New Orleans accent. "Yeah, girl I know you do need a vacation; I need one too . . . me." Many or the New Orleanians had a habit of using a sentence referencing themselves. They always added the word "me" at the end. It was something I could not ever understand.

"Okay Andrea, I'm gonna book my flight for the 26th of April," I said, "but I don't want to leave early in the morning. I will find a flight leaving around 10 or 11 o'clock that morning. I'm not even gonna set myself up booking a flight for 6 o'clock in the morning because I know I will not be at the airport at 5 o'clock in the morning, no not me!" I laughed.

"Tina, you can stay at my house here in Baton Rouge when you get here. My friend will get us a good rate on a hotel in New Orleans for the weekend," Andrea said.

We were both excited because we had not seen each other since she came to visit me in 2003. It had been four years and I really missed not seeing her and her family. We met when I lived and worked in New Orleans in 1997. Andrea later came to work for the company. She worked on the evening program and I helped to train her. We continued to be friends even after the program folded. They survived Hurricane Katrina, but their house was severely damaged from the disaster. Andrea and her Mom relocated to Baton Rouge.

Some trouble started two weeks before I was scheduled to leave. My nephew, Michael Vick, had a cousin, Davon Boddie, who was arrested for allegedly possessing marijuana with the intent to distribute. Davon was Michael's first cousin on his dad's side of the family. He and Michael were very close, and Davon lived in Michael's house that he owned located in Surry County, Virginia. The home was a huge, five bedroom house with lots of space and lots of land surrounding it. Michael had the house built for him and his friends as a bachelor pad.

Well, according to the newspapers, when they checked Davon's identification his address was 2456 Moonlight Road, Surry, Virginia. The police put Davon in jail, it was the talk of the town. After that happened, people who knew members of the Vick Family, began telling us that the Feds (Federal Government Agents) were watching Michael Vick's home.

I remember that approximately four years earlier, Momma and I had conversations with Oogie about hearing some things from other people about dogfighting at the property. We told him about the dangers of dogfighting. We also warned him that people get in trouble with the law for engaging in it. He informed us on that day, "Grandma, I know what I'm doing and I have made good decisions so far and I will continue to make good decisions!" he exclaimed. "I sure hope you will Oopie because the same things that make you happy will make you cry," Momma stated as she sat in her living room chair shaking her head.

My bags were packed and I was ready for New Orleans for my vacation. I called Andrea to let her know I was on my way to the Patrick Henry Airport (known today as the Newport News/ Williamsburg International Airport) for my flight. "Hey Andrea, I'm leaving now and don't forget I'll be in Baton Rouge at 5:59 pm." "Alright girl, I can't wait to see you! I'll be there to get you from the airport!" Andrea said with much excitement. As my son, Felix, and I headed out the door, I set the house alarm, a breaking news story came across the television. I immediately yelled, "Deactivate the alarm Felix! I want to see what has happened to Oogie." Felix replied, "Alright Mom, let me turn the TV volume up." The federal agents had issued a search warrant for Michael Vick's property because of reports of dogfighting. WHAT IN THE WORLD!!!— came to my mind immediately and I realized that the people who informed us about the Feds were actually telling the truth. After watching, we reset the alarm and went out the door, still appalled at the breaking news! I thought, well this is the South, dogfighting is not that big of a deal, so I know he will get out of this. During this time, Michael was the highest paid athlete in the NFL; therefore, I knew he could definitely afford a good legal team to get him out of this. We jumped in my Tahoe sport utility vehicle and headed to the airport.

My total travel time was six hours with the flight change in Atlanta on Airtran Airways. I was so excited about getting to Louisiana and was overwhelmed with joy about the trip. I hadn't been back to the "504" since I lived there. During the flight, I didn't think too much about the news flash I saw on the television because dogfighting had been around for such a long period time.

My Airtran Airways flight was pleasant. I sat next to a man who was a construction manager on his way to Arizona. He and I talked and laughed a lot. Before we knew it, we had talked and laughed during the entire flight. When I got to the baggage claim area, I looked around for Andrea. I was extremely happy to see Andrea and Mrs. Lou-Lou!!! We just grabbed each other and hugged and screamed. We hadn't seen each other in years.

As soon as we got into the car, Andrea said, "Girl, you know it's all over the news around here about Michael, huh."

"Whaaattt," I screamed! I saw a clip of it before I left home," I informed her.

"Yeah girl, they got the federal helicopters flying around his house and everything!!" she said.

I just couldn't wait to get to her house to see what was going on. When I checked my cell phone, I had about seven missed calls. My family had been calling me to talk about all of the breaking news. At the height of his NFL career, our nephew was in trouble with the federal government. WHAT IN THE WORLD WAS HE GOING TO DO???

Once we got to Andrea's house, she turned to ESPN. The story was still breaking news. The reporters kept showing the helicopters flying over Micheal's Surry County home. I really couldn't believe what I was seeing. I was barely able to sleep on my first night in Baton Rouge because I could not get the sound of the helicopters out of my head.

The next day, many of our family members and friends were calling to find out if there was any truth to the story. Friends also called to voice their outrage. They felt like the Feds and the media treated this as if Michael had allegedly killed people instead of dogs. My daughter Tee had moved back to Newport News because she had gotten married. When I talked to her, she said, "The helicopters were everywhere surrounding Oogie's house. Cops were going in the property armed, like in the movies. Dogs were being removed from the property left and right." Tee informed me that she was in shock as she sat holding Shamar, my first grandson and my daughter in law Shameka watched with her mouth wide open. "I'm so glad you're not here Momma," Tee said. "Grandma told that boy about being around all those boys! Grandma tried to tell him!" We could barely finish our conversation because local reporters were calling my cell phone to get comments about the situation. I was glad I didn't have to go to work to deal with the "Mike Vick" haters. Even the well-wishers, at this point, were making things stressful. Even though they were saying they were praying for him, deep down inside, they wanted to know if there was any truth to the story.

I hadn't talked to Oogie. I just wasn't ready to face it all. I told Tee we needed to try to keep it from my momma. She said with all the news coverage, there was no way. Besides, my mother watched the news every day from early morning until the evening news. Her daily ritual consisted of news first at 6 o'clock in the morning. During the commercial breaks, she would read the newspaper and fix her breakfast. Afterwards, she would watch Bob Barker on *The Price Is Right*, then her "stories" as she called them, referring to the soap operas, starting with *The Young and The Restless*.

Despite everything that was going on, I was able to enjoy my week of vacation. Once I returned, my children and I visited my momma. As I watched the news on that day, I was truly amazed at the magnitude of all of the media coverage. Michael came on television and said he did not know what was going on at the house, but he would find out. It seemed like it had been approximately two weeks before he finally made a statement to the public. For several weeks the helicopters kept flying over the house and the *Federal Bureau of Investigation* (FBI) agents was removing from the property the dogs along with the dogfighting equipment.

"He has the worst public relations people," I said as we continued to watch.

"For real, I thought they would have allowed him to make a statement or hold a press conference by now. Wouldn't you Ma?" Tee asked.

"Yes, at least to let people know that's his house. Surely that would reduce some of the speculation," I added.

"You mean to tell me they got this mess on again," Momma said. "I am tired of them showing this mess about Oopie."

"I can't believe they are showing it either, Grandma, because they act like he has killed a lot of people or something," Tee said.

"I know this boy didn't ever think this would happen," Momma commented as she stared at the television and shook her head.

"It's gone be alright Grandma. "It's a shame it has blown way out of proportion," Tee commented.

By the time this incident happened, over half of the Vick Family wasn't talking to each other. People can say money doesn't change families or people, but the money in our case did more harm than good. I had not talked to my sister Brenda in almost three years, nor had I talked to my nephew in over three years. Before the money came in our family, my sister and I had never been mad for any lengthy period of time. The Vick Family hadn't gathered at Momma's house in years. The very place we used to gather to have fun and show great love towards one another was just not the same. Nobody wanted to meet at Momma's house. You would have thought since we were already happy, the money would have made us happier, but that truly wasn't the case.

After this situation kept getting worse and worse, I called Felix to ask him if I should go to Brenda's house. My son Felix was my voice of reason. He always kept a level head and was not biased in his opinions. No matter how mad I was at my family, I didn't want to see my family members in trouble.

I had a bad dream that night. I dreamed Michael was the only one out on the field at the Georgia Dome. He was dressed in his Atlanta Falcons uniform. Out of nowhere someone took a long dagger and threw it out on the field and it went straight into his heart.

When I woke up I was sweating profusely and crying uncontrollably. I could barely catch my breath. I felt nauseated. The dream seemed so real that I put my hand over my eyes to get rid of the images. "Oh my God," I thought. "Is Oogie hurt? Did somebody try to kill him?" I ran upstairs to see if Felix was in his bedroom.

I peeped my head in the door. and said, "Felix, are you up?"

"Yeah Ma, I'm up!" he replied.

"Have you heard from Oogie?" I asked.

He said, "Yeah, why?"

I told Felix about the awful dream and how it seemed so real that I wanted to see if my nephew Oogie was alright. Since we had not spoken in three years, I didn't know how he would react to a call from Auntie Tina.

"Ook is cool Ma; he is not thinking about that stuff right now," Felix said.

The next day I called Tee and told her I was going to Brenda's house to check on them. Tee was pregnant with her first child, Brandon Tyree, and she wanted to go with me. Tee and her high school sweetheart, Brandon had gotten married, earlier that year. It was in the morning on the 4th of August, after Tee's doctor's appointment, that we went over there. I was hoping they would be home.

The ride seemed extremely long. Oogie had bought his mother Brenda a beautiful 8,000 square foot home. The house was made of brick and Hokie Stone on the front and sides. It sat back in a cul-de-sac in The Riverfront subdivision located in Suffolk, Virginia, with a well-manicured front yard. The home had six bedrooms, all of which had private baths. The house also included a mother-in law-suite for our mother. There was even a pool in the back yard. As Tee and I rode through the Merrimac Memorial Bridge-Tunnel, all kinds of thoughts were going through my head.

At this point, the FBI had removed over sixty dogs from the Surry County house. I couldn't believe Oogie had that many dogs located in the back yard. People for the Ethical Treatment of Animals (PETA) representatives and people who didn't like Michael Vick or the Vick Family were pressuring Gerald Poindexter, the Surry County Commonwealth Attorney, to file state charges against Michael. The FBI hauled all kinds of dogfighting training equipment, things most people didn't even know existed, away from the house.

When we arrived, we knocked at the door. "Brenda, Brenda, open the door. It's me and Tee, open up!" I screamed.

"Okay. It's Aunt Tina, Ma," Niki said, as she pulled open the elegant wood and glass door. They were careful about opening the door because of the many strangers who had been coming by the house. One rowdy reporter named, Andy Fox from Channel 10 News, continually went to their house uninvited. He wanted to show the public no one in the Vick Family would come to the door of the house located at West Creek Court.

As I went in, I said nervously, "Hey, Brenda."

"Hey, Tina and Tee ya'll come in," she said and ushered us in the house nervously.

All of us went into the dining room and began hugging each other and crying. "I am so sad about all of this!" I said through my tears.

"I know Aunt Tina, I know, but we'll get through it," Oogie said. He stayed strong and didn't cry. I guess he knew if we saw him crying everybody was going to really break down.

"I can't believe this stuff is going this far!" Tee said as she held Oogie's arm. "There have been many people who have been fighting dogs before you!"

"We didn't want to talk too much on the phone, because we think someone is listening in on our calls," Brenda said.

"Those PETA people keep calling our phone saying real ugly stuff about Ook," Niki explained while drying her tears with her hand.

We all dried our tears and sat around the kitchen table. Tee's stomach was round and Brenda kept rubbing her stomach. We were glad to see each other. The strain from the fame and fortune took its toll on the Vick Family. It was unbelievable.

"Well, I don't care what we've been through; I don't want to see any of my family members in jail," I said as I broke down in tears again. I couldn't stand to see my family going through all of this. Also, the fear of Michael's football career ending was unnerving. We tried to smile and laugh, but with all of the uncertainty—it was hard.

Brenda said, "Oogie you said you wanted the family to start talking again and at least that has happened."

Oogie said with a smile, "Yeah I know, but I sure didn't want it to be like this."

After our visit, things didn't get any better. On August 17th, Michael's other co-defendants, Purnell Price and Quanis Phillips, pleaded guilty to dogfighting charges. They admitted traveling with Michael to host dogfights and described in detail how they "executed approximately eight dogs that did not perform during the testing sessions," according to public records. The other co-defendant, Tony Taylor, pleaded guilty to dogfighting charges at the end of July. He was already in jail. After Michael had tried to remain innocent during the ordeal, on August 23rd, he went to the U.S. District Court in Richmond, Virginia and signed a plea agreement and statement of facts admitting to conspiracy in a dogfighting ring and helping kill pit bulls.

The media showed a close-up shot of Oogie. As he struggled through the crowd, following his attorneys, Billy Martin and Larry Woodard, he managed to get into the court room. Thousands of people were outside waiting to see him. It broke my heart to see him walking in that court house, holding his head up even when he knew he was going down. He had a proud walk, like his Uncle Joe Vick, and he walked with confidence.

The newspapers read:

"Michael 'Ookie' Vick has agreed to plead guilty to a felony charge for his role in the management of a brutal dogfighting ring that was headquartered at a Virginia property owned by the NFL star. Vick, 27, formally entered

his guilty plea today in an appearance at U.S. District Court in Richmond. As part of a plea deal the Atlanta Falcons quarterback admitted that his Bad Newz Kennels operation wagered money—which he provided—in pit bull fights. However, 'Vick didn't gamble by placing side bets on any of the fights,' according to a 'summary of the facts' that was filed today in court. The summary reports that 'Vick did not kill any dogs at this time.'

The plea agreement was 22 pages. This was the top story in the news.

Even though I always knew he had dogs, with this statement, there was no more guessing for me, the rest of the Atlanta football fans or the rest of the nation. Michael was going down for some damn dogs. "What the hell!" I said as I watched the television. "This is sad."

The next day, NFL commissioner Roger Goodell told the media that the information in the plea agreement was not the same story Michael had told them. It was suspect that Goodell likely would suspend Michael indefinitely. A final decision on his suspension would be made after his legal case is resolved. "We totally condemn the conduct outlined in the charges, which is inconsistent with what Michael Vick previously told both our office and the Atlanta Falcons," the NFL Commissioner stated. The league, which barred Michael from training camp, said it asked the Falcons to withhold further action until the NFL's internal investigation wrapped up. "The commissioner has not decided on a specific timetable regarding Michael Vick's status."

"The Falcons said they were "certainly troubled" by news of the plea, but would withhold further comment in compliance with Goodell's request. If the league suspends Michael, the Falcons could then seek to recoup part of his signing bonus of approximately $22 million, because if suspended, then Michael would be in default of his contract," team officials told ESPN's Sal Paolantonio. Then the next day, NFL Commissioner Roger Goodell suspended Vick indefinitely without pay.

Michael held a press conference and I could see the sadness in his eyes. He had gone from looking like a person I wasn't that familiar with, the braids and tattoos, back to looking like the young man excited about his opportunity, an avid listener who wanted to do the right things. "I accept responsibility for my actions," he said. "I want to apologize to all of the people I hurt by participating in this."

He could be sentenced "six years for some dogfighting," I mumbled to myself. That's a damn shame." The reports said up to six years and it could incur a $250,000 fine. I shook my head as I stared at the television in my bedroom, sifting through unwanted papers.

I called my girlfriend Carolyn. "Are you looking at television?" I asked.

She answered, "Yeah girl. I can't believe what they are saying about your nephew. I can't believe it, six years for some dogs?"

"Yeah, up to six years, and Vice President Dick Cheney shot a person when he was out hunting and he didn't even get arrested," I said.

Carolyn replied, "And people used to do dogfighting down in North Carolina where Daddy lives. And if society is going to complain about cruelty to animals, they need to start with the horse racing and what they do to those poor animals. They inject them with steroids in their early years and put a lot of wear and tear on the horses. If they don't win races, they put them to sleep. They won't say anything about that because people are making money off of it!" Carolyn was an avid horse lover.

"Well, I know you know about that," I said.

"Yeah, I have seen that go on for years, not to mention the PETA employees a few years ago in North Carolina," Carolyn added.

"I remember that and I don't even know if they ever got any time," I said.

"The case didn't make a big deal like this one with Michael," she said.

"Well Carolyn, I gotta go and meet this man about my laptop computer," I said.

"Okay, keep me posted, Tina," she said.

I collected my money and went to meet Diane's co-worker, Mr. Ken, who worked on computers. I took my laptop to see if he could show me how to adjust it for wireless. We sat at his kitchen table while he made the adjustments. He told me I would need a wireless router at home in order to go wireless. As soon as the internet connected, there flashed the story of "Michael Vick Tests Positive for Marijuana." I was so embarrassed that I just grabbed my computer and left. I got in my car and began crying. "Can the Vick Family situation get any worse?" I asked myself.

During the month of October, my co-worker Michele Grant and I were scheduled to attend an affordable housing conference in Chicago, Illinois. I debated about attending this conference, but I needed to get out of town. Everywhere I went there was talk about dogfighting. It was our first trip to the "windy city." I was glad to get away not only for the conference, but to get away from the dogfighting saga. The City of Chicago, of course, was synonymous with Oprah. Unfortunately, we were unsuccessful in getting tickets to the show before we arrived in the city.

After the two and a half days of the conference were over, we had one more day before we were to head back to Virginia. Can you imagine actually being in Chicago and not seeing Oprah Winfrey? That night, I went to the concierge of the Knickerbocker Millennium Hotel where we were staying.

"Do you have tickets to the Oprah Show?" I asked the concierge.

"Just wait one second miss, I'll check," the concierge said.

"I have been trying to get tickets on-line, but it hasn't worked," I said.

"Oh no, well let me see what I can do," the concierge said.

The concierge picked up the phone and dialed a number. Of course I thought this was a joke and this was the protocol they went through when their guests asked for tickets. When the concierge began talking with someone at the show, small beads of sweat began to form on my forehead. The concierge hung up the phone and gave me two passes to the Oprah Show hotel standby line and informed me that it was a 90% chance that we would get in to see the show. "Oh my God!!! Thank you!!!" I yelled and tipped the concierge and rushed upstairs to let Michele know what we needed to do.

The next morning we got a taxi and headed directly to Harpo Studios. Needless to say, we were the first people to arrive in the hotel standby line. Since the dogfighting saga was going on, I was careful about saying my last name.

"Michele, I'm not telling anyone my last name because they might ask me to be on the show," I told her.

"I know," she laughed.

I replied, "All they need to know is my name is Tina."

"Good Morning ladies and welcome to Harpo Studios," the security guard said.

"Good Morning," we replied.

"Where are you ladies from?" he said.

Michele and I looked at each other and I let her answer. "We are visiting from Virginia," Michele said.

"Well, we are glad you came to visit us."

The temperature began dropping; the lines were forming; people were talking to one another, and before we knew it, yes, you guessed it, we were in the studio!!!

The studio production specialist announced the guest for the taping. It was Dr. Oz. I like Dr. Oz, but I have to be perfectly honest, I was hoping for Jamie Foxx or Denzel Washington. But, since we were fortunate enough to get passes, I definitely didn't want to complain. They taped two episodes in the hours we were there. However, the second taping was about a professor at Carnegie Mellon University by the name of Randy Pausch. He had composed his last lecture because he was dying from pancreatic cancer. He only had a few months to live. At the end of his lecture, he stated that he had actually made the tape so that his three young children would have some direction from him on life's lessons once he was gone.

The points that Professor Pausch highlighted in his presentation were great. He put into words, what so many people who are successful practice daily. He discussed working hard to achieve your dreams, being humble, and not giving up. In a segment of the lecture, Pausch stated, "The brick walls that are in our way are not there to keep us out, but to give us a way to show how much we really want something." It is unfortunate Professor Pausch will probably not get the opportunity to see his children become adults. As the old folks used to say, "The doctors can say no, but God has the final say."

As I sat there, I thought that all of us should be sitting in front of a recorder and formulating our last lecture. Although Professor Pausch was given a time frame from the doctor as to how much longer he had to live, the truth of the matter is that all of our lives will expire. No one was given any guaranteed certificate when they were born that said, "You'll stay on earth forever." It's so important we take time with our children to tell them about our lives, the downs as well as the ups and the life lessons we have learned. So many times as adults, we want to hide some of the not-so-good decisions we made in our past, but our mistakes help our children understand that we are human.

As we left the studio, the lecture remained in my mind. I repeatedly thanked God for allowing me to live and enjoy my two wonderful children as they grew up. As a single parent, I had to work, but I took jobs with lower wages so that I could be at home or on my way home when they were getting out of school. I wanted to spend time with them. Just listening to Professor Pausch made me proud of the decisions I made to take care of my family.

These days, I see many parents who would much rather go to parties and take trips every weekend while leaving someone else to care for their children. When parents have children, they have to make choices. The choices should include prioritizing time for your children, not getting out of the house to get to the next party.

As Oprah finished her interviews, she came down the walkway to leave the set. I stood up to shake her hand. "Oprah, we love you in Virginia!" I screamed. She looked at me and chanted, "Thank you!" Being a longtime Oprah admirer, I have to say the trip was well worth it. Michele and I could not believe our Oprah experience.

The next day we were back in Virginia. The Michael Vick saga was the last thing I wanted to deal with, especially after such an empowering trip to Chicago. Oogie kept saying he had talked to the attorneys and that he would probably get anywhere from four to six months, instead of serving six years. In November, the Vick Family gathered at his Hampton, Virginia home to have what seemed to us like the "last supper." Oogie made the decision to turn himself in to the U.S. Marshall earlier than his scheduled court date. We all pleaded with him to stay at least until Thanksgiving, but he insisted on leaving earlier. Brenda prepared a nice dinner with all of her son's favorite dishes. The dinner included lasagna, turkey and dressing, and collard greens. All of us sat around and talked and tried to cheer each other up. Michael assured us he would be back home in approximately six months.

On December 9th I called Brenda to see how she was doing. She couldn't stop crying, knowing that her son was headed to federal prison. "I'll just be glad when all of this is over," Brenda said. "I can't stand seeing my baby in jail; I just can't take it."

"Brenda, I won't be in court because I have to work, but I will keep all of you in my prayers because this is hard to deal with and very hurtful," I said.

The next day they headed to the Federal Court in Richmond, Virginia. Brenda, her children and the rest of the family went to court in support of Michael. Oogie's pastor, Pastor Kelley of Psalms Ministries and hundreds of Vick supporter's crowded around the courtroom. There were many opponents present. These included PETA and a host of animal lovers who if they had their way, they would have convicted him as soon as he stepped into the courtroom.

My soror Bonita Towner lived in the Henrico County area, but she worked in Richmond, Virginia. "Good morning Tina, this is Bonita," she said with a sad sounding tone.

"Good Morning Bonita," I said.

"How are you doing?" she asked.

"Not too good today, girl," I said. "You know Michael, well we call Michael, Oogie, goes to court this morning."

"Yes, Tina they have all of the streets blocked off in Richmond around Main Street and Government Street because of all of the media and the people here," Bonita said. "You would have thought Charlie Manson was on trial in Richmond. It is so many people outside, we had to come to work early just so we could get in our office building. You know my office is only a block from the courthouse. One of my co-workers went out in the crowd to see if he could see Michael and take some pictures of the crowd," she added.

"Girl, what? Is it that many people out there!?" I asked loudly.

"Yes, people are everywhere, some holding up signs against Michael, but a lot of people holding up signs supporting him," she informed me.

"Well, let me turn my television on so I can see exactly what is going on?" I replied.

"Okay Tina let me get to work. I'll call you later."

I got off of the telephone and turned the television to ESPN. They had full coverage of the sentencing. I was able to prepare for work and watch the coverage. I had one TV on in my bedroom and another one on in the living room. As I got dressed for work, I could watch what was happening on either of the TV sets. From what I watched, you could see all of the people outside of the court and even the mass media circus. It looked as if every network in America had someone outside with their satellites and mass media equipment covering the case. People had signs with messages such as "ConVick Michael Vick" and "NFL Sacks Vick." The glimmer of hope for me was when I looked in the crowd, and there was a little boy who looked to be about eight or nine years old, with his head held high and his sign up in the air that read, "Keep the Faith #7."

All of our family members dreaded turning on our television sets because we were so sick of the breaking news about the dogfighting. Every fifteen minutes there was an update of Michael Vick and the dogfighting situation. I loved my nephew Oogie, the Baby Woo, whom had been in my life since he was born. He had worked hard and stayed focused, and here he was now about to end his career and on his way to federal prison. I'm not minimizing the crime because I have owned a dog for many years. Before my Mother's death, she would watch the news and say, "I can't believe this boy done went from the NFL to the jailhouse!" Tears were in her eyes because she loved all of her children and grandchildren, and hated seeing all of this happen to her superstar grandson. My heart hurt so badly for a young man who was a part of my family. Michael had the same bloodline as me because of his Mom, my sister Brenda, who was going through all of this over a challenging decision he made which we could clearly see had taken a turn for the worst. "Oogie what in the world has happened??" I kept thinking over and over in my mind. "Wow, federal prison!"

I took my curlers out of my hair and walked from the bedroom to the living room, I stared at the television. The ESPN reporter struggled to put in his ear piece as he received the verdict and appeared shaken in disbelief as he stated the following nervously: "It appears they have given Michael Vick 23 months for his sentencing." "What!" I screamed in total disbelief!! "Twenty three months!!! I collapsed to my knees and began crying profusely. "I can't believe this," I sobbed, "I thought Oogie said four to six months."

I immediately picked up the phone and called my Momma. I could barely dial her number because my fingers and hands were shaking uncontrollably.

"Hello." Momma said when she answered the phone.

"Ma, are you looking at the news?" I screamed. "They done gave Oogie 23 months! I just can't believe this!" I screamed.

"Yeah Tina, I'm so upset, I just can't believe, Oopie is in jail!" she said.

"I wonder what happened Ma, cuz Oogie said he wouldn't get but four to six months."

"I don't know," Momma responded.

Momma was strong. She wasn't crying, at least not on the outside, but I knew she was on the inside. Momma had been through many trials in her life. I believe she had chosen not to cry, just so we wouldn't be more upset. Even through all of the things she went through with Daddy, I had never seen her cry. She just somehow figured out what to do next. I truly admired her strength and was so glad she was around. She always made everything better.

I managed to calm down and get my emotions together. When I got off of the phone and went back to watching the news, I saw the sketches of the courtroom scenes. My heart was crushed looking at the pictures of my sister, Brenda, with her head held down because she was too weak to look up. Marcus, was right there beside his Mom holding her and helping her to make it through this awful tragedy. I cringed at the sight of Michael Vick, in a black and white jail outfit. I called Brenda when I thought they were out of court, but her phone went straight to voicemail. Then, I called Marcus. Marcus was outraged and he told the lawyers they better give his brother his money back because he felt like they should have done more. My deeper thoughts were that if the renowned attorney, Johnny Cochran was alive, Michael would have gotten perhaps less time and probably not gotten any time in the federal prison.

Michael couldn't make this go away. The presiding Judge, U.S. District Judge Henry E. Hudson, let everyone know that during Michael Vick's case, he received the most letters he had ever received during his time serving as a judge. "I'm not convinced you've fully accepted responsibility," The Honorable Hudson said to Michael. Despite Michael's early surrender, his public apology and participation in an animal sensitivity training course, he was completely denied an "acceptance of responsibility" credit that would have reduced his sentence. The federal prosecutors, including Michael Gill, did not want Michael to get the credit. It was over. Michael was going to jail for almost two years. It all seemed like a dream. It was unbelievable that someone who had never had a criminal history, not even as a juvenile, got close to two years for killing eight dogs. They acted as if Michael invented dogfighting, but we knew the legal system was using him as an example.

People called all day long to say they were praying for our family. There were so many people calling Brenda that she had to turn her phone off. This whole dogfighting scenario was a "dreaded revelation" that turned ultimately into a tragic day for the entire Vick Family.

CHAPTER TEN

THE COMEBACK

"Lord we are praying, right now, in the name of Jesus. We ask that you make a way for our nephew, Michael Vick," Joe Jr. prayed, as we held hands. We were in my real estate office on 27th Street and Chestnut Avenue. It was a small office in downtown Newport News located in the Chestnut Avenue Business Corridor. "We pray, Lord, that you will allow Oogie a second chance," Joe Jr. said as he continued to pray. "Let thy will be done and let one of the NFL teams choose him as their quarterback," he said. "We love you, Lord, and we know you are a way maker." Joe Jr. could always pray. He believed in the power of prayer and read his Bible every morning. Joe Jr. knew the word because when he went to jail, he read every chapter of the Holy Bible. He had much faith. After we prayed Joe Jr. said, "God is going to take care of everything, sis."

Although Joe Jr. had his issues, he was one of the nicest people anyone could ever meet. One time, when Joe Jr. was roaming on the Newport News streets of Marshall Avenue, he saw a house on fire and the family was struggling to get out. He went to help rescue the people and took them to safety. His picture was in our local newspaper denoting him as a "hero." We were proud of him. One of my friends, Anya Rose, just loved Joe Jr. She would tell everybody, "Girl, one day I had locked my keys in the car and girl, I was glad to see Joe Vick coming down the street. He took the coat hanger and stretched it out and kept wiggling it until the lock popped open," she said while laughing every time she told that story. I love my brother Joe Jr. We shared some of the best times together. He was affectionately known in the Vick Family as "the peace maker."

Despite my brother Joe Jr. having difficulty getting his life together, he was the most forgiving person anyone could ever want to meet. I would sometimes compare our lives. When I thought about how I was faithful in keeping a job and raising my family, but if I got mad at someone, I could stay mad forever and would not think about forgiving. I always felt like God would let my brother in Heaven before me just because he was adamant about the power of forgiveness.

During this period in time, we were nervous because about four teams had already stated they did not want to take a chance on hiring Michael Vick. His troubles off of the field were affecting his chances to do what he loved—playing football. Michael had been released from prison and the NFL commissioner did allow him to become eligible to play football again. It was just a matter of who would choose him to be a part of their team. As a result of the dogfighting, Michael had two groups of followers: group one who believed the dogfighting had been taken to the extreme and Michael was used as an example; and group two who thought he should be crucified and never have another chance to play in the NFL.

The next day, Oogie called around to tell us that the Philadelphia Eagles located in Philadelphia "Philly", Pennsylvania were considering giving him a chance on their team. He knew everyone was worried about him. God really did hear our prayers.

All of the family was happy Oogie got a second chance. We called each other to say how magnificent it was that Coach Andy Reid and the owner had given Michael a chance to come back and do what he has always done best—play football. I knew he had done wrong with the dogfighting, but was it fair to take his opportunity to play football again? He had already lost almost everything.

The PETA organization became very vocal again. Their representatives said Michael Vick needed to have a psychiatric evaluation before he could play again. I was appalled and extremely mad about what they were requesting. My sister Brenda was still distraught about all of the matters concerning her son. My position was to hold a press conference to let the PETA representatives and everyone who agreed with them know that the judge had given him his time and he had served it. PETA needed to leave my nephew ALONE!!!

Michael's girlfriend Kijafa Frink had been dating him for years and during the entire time she stood by his side. Kijafa was a beautiful and good business woman who was also an excellent cook. She was attending Hampton University when she met my nephew. Kijafa and her family were from Philadelphia, Pennsylvania.

Once the NFL deal, concerning Michael becoming a player on the Philadelphia Eagles team, was negotiated and executed, he was delighted and happy about having a second chance. For him, it just wasn't about the money; it was about him wanting a chance to do what he loved—play football. Even though he did not play in the first few games, he texted me to let me know he would be starting in the seventh game of the season.

The Vick Family went to Philly for the Sunday afternoon game. We went to Oogie and Kijafa's home a few hours before the game.

I hugged Oogie tightly and said, "I am glad we can put this behind us."

"I know, me too," Oogie said.

On that particular day, he didn't talk much. and he wasn't loud like we were. We were happy to be there, and his daughters Jada and London were jumping and flipping around the house.

"Ya'll act just like ya'll grandma when she was little," I said. Brenda used to love to do flips and jump around when Momma had company. "I should say, your Daddy too. Michael used to do somersaults and all kinds of flips when he was little." I told them. When he was flipping too much, Momma used to say, "Okay Oopie, don't make me get that fly swatter." Everyone started laughing. It was as if we could hear Momma's voice. She would threaten him with the fly swatter, when she knew she was not going to use it.

Later we headed to the Philadelphia Eagles' game, at the Lincoln Financial Field Stadium. As an elected official, I could not help but notice the economic impact of having such a stadium. The real estate tax income would generate such a venture was my first thought. The revenue from food and drink sales was thought number two. The amount of people employed at the stadium, made me contemplate whether the State of Virginia could support something of this magnitude? It had the seating capacity of approximately 68,000 with 172 luxury suites with the seating capacity of approximately 3,000. A few years earlier, the total renovation of Lincoln Financial Field was $512 million. There were several restrooms and two 27' x 96' video screens, which featured advertisements from the sponsors for the games. Oogie had us seated in what was called a "box." It was one of the luxury suites he purchased for his family and close friends. The box was very nice, but I really liked being in the crowd with all of the Philadelphia fans.

The Philadelphia Eagles and the Minnesota Vikings were out on the field warming up for the start of the game. All of us were cheering the Eagles on. I was so proud of Oogie and his comeback. Since it was the Eagle's home game, the announcer called the line up for the Vikings first. We all were eagerly awaiting the call for our Vick Family star, Michael Vick. After approximately three years, all of us were excited and ready to see Oogie back on the field. It was unbelievable to have someone you have known since birth become a big superstar!

It was time for the Eagle's starting line-up. There was a tunnel where all of the players came through as they left the locker room. All of Michael's supporting cast, which was the first string of players, came out one-by-one as the announcer called their names. Then the announcer said, "And our Eagles' quarterback—Michael Vick!" The crowd went utterly wild! I stared from the box, looking at him run out of the tunnel wearing his "#7" jersey. As Michael ran out, he put his fist in the air. The spectators clapped and screamed even louder! It was a thunderous applause! My nephew had made it through his dogfighting saga. Now, he had another chance at the life he loved—**FOOTBALL**.

I screamed, then tears came to my eyes. I was so very proud of, Michael Vick, for being able to withstand everything he went through. The strength he had truthfully came from his experiences of growing up in a family that made its own way. Through my tears, I wished Momma could be there to see her grandson Oopie. She would have been extremely proud of the thousands of fans who forgave him and filled Lincoln Financial Field Stadium to see **MICHAEL VICK'S COMEBACK!!!**

CHAPTER ELEVEN

THE POLITICS CONTINUE

The politics of the City of Newport News were difficult. I was approaching the end of my first term. I honestly considered not running for the seat anymore because of what I had witnessed the first four years. It was difficult for me to see the injustices each day against communities because of race, gender and class structure. It troubled me to see how many of the leaders who claimed to be out for the people's best interest were not.

Our official title was "The Honorable City Council." One night as I sat in my kitchen, drinking my vodka and tonic, I thought seriously about our titles. I was having a difficult time seeing what was really honorable about this job, especially after an incident when one of the council members got up out of his seat to hit one of my female colleagues. After that incident, I contemplated submitting my letter of resignation for the city council. To see this man get up out of his seat to attack this woman, like some thug on the street, was utterly ridiculous. I hoped he wouldn't hit her, as he stood over her with his fists clinched. I had worked with juvenile offenders for ten years and I had never been in a meeting, in all of my professional life, where anything like this had happened. It was also disheartening, to meet so many male leaders who didn't think women should have an opinion, let alone, voice one. Not only that, a city where there is a group of wealthy men who want to control government and their agenda does not include fairness and justice for all. And, it definitely didn't include improving the South District, which I represented.

I was undecided about what to do. However, when I heard not one, but three rumors that some unqualified people wanted to take my seat, it sparked me to get recharged. Part of the plan included the "establishment" wanting to unseat me because I was vocal about the improvements I wanted in the South District. They didn't want the blacks on council to talk or have any ideas. You had to be a "rubber stamp" and do whatever "the establishment" told you to do. I knew they were not going to take my seat, mainly because of my outstanding accomplishments in such a short time. In only one four year term, I had worked to get support for the Noland Green Apartments, Heritage Forrest Apartments, Dr. Martin Luther King Jr. Plaza, a new Walmart and funding to improve our Lower Jefferson Avenue Corridor. I also wanted to remain in office to see the creation of the New Apprentice School project, which I voted to support with the rest of my colleagues. The new school would be an asset to the Shipyard, which was one of our city's largest employers.

There were also other ideas I wanted to continue working on to improve the conditions of the community. My business partner, Delphine White and I continued to search for investors for our Whittaker Heritage Housing Development. Delphine was a savvy business woman who had come here to Hampton Roads by way of Newport Beach, California. She was six feet tall with blonde hair and hazel eyes. She worked as an environmental specialist and had earned lots of money. She came to Virginia looking for investments.

Our plan was to have apartments for veterans. It involved the rehabilitation of an 80,000 square foot building into 80 individual apartments for veterans. The extra space would be office space for on-site services, such as mental health support, job readiness and security. The old hospital sat on the corner of 28th Street and Orcutt Avenue. It had been financed in the 1940's by progressive blacks. The building was designed by a black architect, by the name of William Moses. It was built during the era of segregation, and a time when blacks had to go to the jails for healthcare. They were not allowed in the white hospitals.

I still had much excitement working with Professor Natalie Robertson who also owned her own building on the corner of 22nd Street and Wickham Avenue. The entire place was 10,000 square feet and Dr. Robertson had the vision to renovate it and create a job training facility. I admired and supported her vision because, once renovated, it would enhance the community since people in the neighborhood were disconnected from jobs and job training. I knew the impact of having a job training facility in the neighborhood. Citizens could at least have the advantage of getting direction for a job and career.

Natalie was also a professor at Hampton University. She wanted to give back to the community. Natalie was extremely smart and already had the building gutted out when I met her. My friend Tommy Garner who owned Tommy Garner Air Conditioning & Heating Company was generous enough to donate a heating system to help us get started. Tommy and I attended high school together. He had become a successful businessman. Tommy shared my vision in trying to improve the lives of the people in the community.

Being a woman business owner myself, I was elated to support female-owned businesses in the area. One of my high school friends, Renita Bland Parker, had started an organization named "Good Seed Good Ground." Her organization helped poor people get a hand up. God had given her the ability to work with the underprivileged. Along with her husband Chris, she helped many young people find jobs. She assisted people in filling out applications, resumes and interviewing skills. Renita was connected to many employers in the Williamsburg area. They bought a bus to be able to transport people to jobs in Williamsburg. Renita and I also worked together on several job fairs. All of the employers who registered with our job fair were required to have positions available. The last two years of the job fair in downtown Newport News had record numbers of people who wanted to work. It really showed me that if people have an opportunity, they will take it.

I had a good track record, and I wanted my work to continue. Months went by and the rumors kept circulating. I wasn't worried, because I was ready for any opponents. I was confident about my community and I had a great campaign team. In February of 2012, I declared my candidacy for re-election. We started with my "50th Birthday Bash and Campaign Kick-Off." Many of the business men and lawyers in the city who knew I just wanted the best for my community did support me financially. They didn't want me penalized for wanted to do what citizens expected of their leadership. The Vick Team canvassed the neighborhoods on Saturdays for weeks. I worked hard to raise money and my true supporters helped me financially. I outworked my opponents in the neighborhoods. I was glad to see citizens who would see me and say, "Thank you, Councilwoman Vick for standing for us. We definitely see a change in our community." Those are the priceless compliments that strengthen me and keep me fighting for a better community.

The results were in on the night of May 1, 2012. My supporters and campaign workers were all at my house for the **VICKTORY** party! I stomped my opponents for a second term and continued my life in politics.

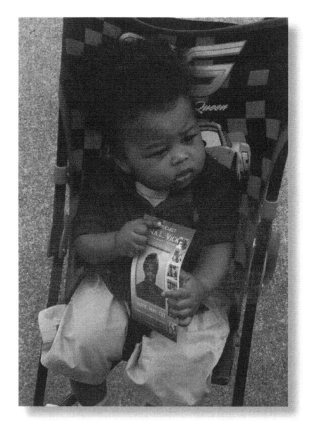

My grandson #3 Tyson Carter supporting his Grandma Tina

BOOK CREDITS

"Daily Press"

CNN sportsillustrated.cnn.com/football/college/1999/bowls/sugar/ news, "Sugar Bowl Notebook"

Wikipedia, The Boxcar Children

About The Author

Ms. Vick is the aunt of NFL Superstar Quarterback Michael Vick, a business women, and an elected official. She was Born and raised in Newport News, Virginia in the southeast community by the late Joseph and Caletha Vick. She was educated in the city's public school system. In 1984, Ms. Vick received her Bachelor of Science Degree in Communications from Virginia Commonwealth University in Richmond, Virginia. She also completed the Alpha College of Real Estate in 2001.

Ms. Vick returned to her Newport News community and has since been active in working to make changes in the community. For five years, she worked as Director for Peninsula Community Development Corporation (PCDC), where she created a homebuyers club to educate hundreds of community residents about the homeownership process. Under Ms. Vick's leadership, the department renovated and built new construction homes in the southeast community and in the city of Hampton to promote efforts to eliminate the city's blight and unsafe neighborhoods. She has also been instrumental in educating and finding affordable homes for first time homebuyers.

Ms. Vick continues to work with potential homebuyers, but now in a different capacity: principal broker and owner of Tina L. Vick Realty & Development, LLC., located in Newport News. She was elected to serve on the Newport News City Council in 2008. She is the proud mother of daughter, Teunsha Vick and her son, Terrance Vick and grandmother to Shamar Vick, Tyree Diggs and Tyson Carter. Ms. Vick can be reached at www.growingupvick.com.

Edwards Brothers Malloy
Oxnard, CA USA
January 20, 2016